Heart-Made The Cutting-Edge of Chinese Contemporary Architecture

Heart-Made
The Cutting-Edge of Chinese Contemporary Architecture

FRONT COVER: **'URBAN FOREST'** ARCHITECT: Ma Yansong / MAD
BACK COVER: **OCT ART AND DESIGN GALLERY** ARCHITECT: Urbanus
OPPOSITE: **'SUPERSTAR: A MOBILE CHINATOWN'** ARCHITECT: Ma Yansong / MAD

Programme and Organization

MINISTRY OF CULTURE OF THE PEOPLE'S REPUBLIC OF CHINA -
Bureau of External Cultural relations; City of Beijing; City of Shanghai;
Province of Jiangsu; Province of Guangdong; NAMOC - National Art
Museum of P.R.C.; China International Exhibitions Agency; SACH - State
Administration of Cultural Heritage of P.R.C.; CPAA - China Performing
Arts Agency; Chinese Writers' Association; Film Bureau / China Film
Archive; CFLAC - China's Federation of Literary & Art Circles | and their
cultural partners in the People's Republic of China

Hong Kong SAR and its cultural partners

Europalia International aisbl and its numerous cultural partners in
Belgium and in the neighbouring countries

Funding
We would like to thank
In Belgium
FPS Foreign Affairs
Belgian Science Policy
FPS employment

Vlaamse Gemeenschap
Communauté française de Belgique
Brussels Capital Region
Deutschsprachige Gemeinschaft
National Lottery
BEKAERT
GDF-SUEZ
HAINAN AIRLINES
TOTAL

National Bank of Belgium
ING
Solvay

Régie des bâtiments | Regie der Gebouwen
BARCO
Procon
Deloitte
Toyota
Thon Hotels
Thalys

De Standaard
La Libre Belgique
Knack / Le Vif L'Express
Canvas / Klara
La Deux / La Première / Musiq'3

With the support of
In Belgium
Embassy of the People's Republic of China
Mission of the People's Republic of China to European communities
Chancellery of the Prime Minister
FPS Foreign Affairs
Hong Kong Economic and Trade Office Belgium
Belgium-Chinese Chamber of Commerce
Flanders-China Chamber of Commerce

In the People's Republic of China
Embassy of Belgium
Consuls generals

Working committee in the People's Republic of China
DONG Junxin
General Commissioner europalia.china

FAN Di'an
General Curator of the exhibitions

WANG Hui
Project Manager for the programme organized by the city of Beijing.
Director Information Office of the People's Government of Beijing
Municipality

LIU Wenguo
General Project Manager for the programme organized by the city
of Shanghai. Deputy Director, Shanghai Municipal Administration
of Culture, Radio, Film and TV

YU Qikeng
Deputy Director of the Guangdong Provincial Department of Culture

ZHANG Jinhua
General Director, Jiangsu Province Department of Culture.
Deputy Director of Publicity Department Jiangsu Province

CHEN Ping
Director of the festival europalia.china

YAN Dong
General coordination of exhibitions

WANG Xiuqin
General coordination of performing arts

ZHAO Xinshu
Head of exhibitions

WANG Meng
Head of press and communication

LIU Chengcheng
Head of performing arts, film and literature

WANG Ying, ZHENG Yan, LIU Chunfeng
Exhibitions

TAN Ziqiang, ZHU Dan
Performing arts

4

Heart-Made
The Cutting-Edge of Chinese Contemporary Architecture

EXHIBITION
This exhibition was organized by the International Centre for Urbanism, Architecture and Landscape (CIVA), in partnership with Espace architecture La Cambre Horta, within the scope of europalia.china

15 October 2009 – 21 February 2010

Curators
Fang Zhenning
Christophe Pourtois
Marcelle Rabinowicz

Communications
Véronique Moerman, assisted by **Andrea Flores**

Sponsorship
Myriam Degauque

Assembly
Renaud De Staercke
Mohamed Houlliche
Christophe Méaux
and the entire **CIVA team**

Acknowledgements
The organizers would like to thank the following
The Ministry of Culture of the People's Republic of China
The China International Exhibition Agency
The National Art Museum of China
Abitare China
FANG Media Studio
i-FANG Design

Chen Ping, Fan Di'an, Zhang Yu, Yan Dong, Liu Zhenlin, Wang Ying, Jiang He, Hou Zhimin, Zheng Yan, Sun Vittorio, Xu Li, Zhang Daping, Lin Fanyu, Zhong Guangli, Zhang Hui, Chen Shuyu

And all the architects and artists who kindly participated in this project
L'Espace architecture La Cambre Horta
Marc Kohen, Délégué de la Communauté française de Belgique et de la Région wallonne
Christine Simon
Sophia Zhang
Brussels Export and its representatives

CIVA
The Board of Directors chaired by **Marie Vanhamme**

With support from
La Communauté française de Belgique
La Commission communautaire française
The Brussels-Capitale Region
The Federal Science Policy Office
The Ixelles College of Burgomasters and **Deputy Burgomasters**

And with the help of
The National Lottery, Sigma Coatings, Invicta

EUROPALIA
Kristine De Mulder
Dirk Vermaelen
Astrid Beauduin

CATALOGUE
The catalogue has been published to accompany the exhibition of the same name.
The texts published in this catalogue are entirely the responsibility of their authors.

Authors
Fang Zhenning
Christophe Pourtois
Marcelle Rabinowicz

Publishers
Europalia International, CIVA and **Fonds Mercator**

Production and editorial coordination
Laurent Germeau, Brussels, for Fonds Mercator

Translation of 'Beyond the Contemporary'
John Wright

Editing
Kate Bell, Marcelline Bosquillon, John Wright

Graphic design and typesetting
Dojo Design, Brussels
Typeface TSTAR

Printing and binding
Snel Grafics sa, Vottem
Paper G-Print 170 g, Grycksbo Paper

www.civa.be   www.fondsmercator.be   www.europalia.eu

ISBN 978 90 6153 894 3 – D/2009/703/41

Contents

Espace architecture La Cambre Horta

INVICTA ART

SIGMA COATINGS

FANG Media   i-FANG

Europalia International

Europalia International is an international non-profit association, which aims to promote cultural heritages by holding the Europalia Festival. Launched in Brussels in 1969, the name Europalia comes from a combination of two words – Europe and Opalia (the Roman festival celebrating a rich harvest). Europalia is held every two years in Brussels and other Belgian towns, including frontier regions, and runs for several months. This multidisciplinary festival illustrates all aspects of the art and culture of European or non-European countries. With the aim of promoting understanding between the nations, the partner country of each festival is given the opportunity to show its cultural heritage in the widest possible way. Europalia hopes, in this way, to raise the cultural and educational importance of Europe and confirm the role of Belgium and Brussels, the capital of the European Union. This year, from 8 October 2009 until 14 February 2010, Europalia will devote its festival to China.

More information on www.europalia.eu

HEART-MADE The Cutting-Edge of Chinese Contemporary Architecture

CLAIRE KIRSCHEN, GENERAL COMMISSIONER
EUROPALIA.CHINA BELGIUM

Europalia International is celebrating this year its 40th anniversary and has established an extensive network of correspondents all over Europe and Belgium. It has acquired a worldwide reputation and is today ranked among the most important festivals in Europe.

By devoting this twenty-second Europalia Festival to China, the President of the People's Republic of China, Hu Jintao, and HM the King of the Belgians, have opened up new perspectives of cultural cooperation between Europalia and Chinese culture in all its diversity and dynamic evolution.

Anybody looking at the skyline of the Chinese countryside, and even more so in the cities, will feel some dizziness at the speed with which it has changed in recent years. How far will it go? Will all traces of ancient China – the *hutongs* in Beijing and the round Hakka *tulou* buildings in the south – be completely erased in the future? A new generation of young Chinese architects and artists have been formulating their own original views and reactions to these various challenges. On the occasion of europalia.china, the CIVA presents an exhibition of plans, models, animations, videos and soundworks revealing how the men and women of this generation are approaching the future with their 'hearts', seeking to contribute a more humane dimension to the society of their dreams.

Europalia would like to express its gratitude to Fang Zhenning, the Chinese curator of this exhibition, and to Fan Di'an, the Chinese General Curator for exhibitions and Director of the National Art Museum of China. Yan Dong, Deputy Director and Liu Zhenlin, Wang Ying and Jiang He from China International Exhibitions Agency have also provided invaluable contributions to this initiative, which has benefited from the professional and experienced assistance of Christophe Pourtois and Marcelle Rabinowicz at the CIVA.

The Ministry of Culture of the People's Republic of China has contributed an enormous effort to ensure that europalia.china will be a festival of exceptional importance and diversity. Under the guidance of the General Commissioner, Dong Junxin, it has been possible to establish strong ties of friendship and solidarity with the Belgian Europalia team. We would like to take this opportunity to express to them our heartfelt gratitude.

Beyond the Contemporary

CHRISTOPHE POURTOIS, MARCELLE RABINOWICZ, CIVA

The Middle Kingdom's relatively abrupt emergence from a decades-long isolation has thrust its urban profile – without any transitional period – into the era of globalization. The architectural movements that initially dominated the West and then spread to the rest of the planet had little influence on China between the 1930s and the beginning of the 1990s. Modernist and Post-Modernist styles found hardly any echo until China's recent opening up.

China has been confronted by major urban planning challenges, namely how to handle an accelerated process of urbanization for a population that, until quite recently, had been essentially a rural one. In order to respond to a legitimate demand for better housing conditions, the country has organized itself on a number of levels with the goal of finding appropriate responses.

Firstly, the welcome extended towards internationally recognized architects has allowed for a certain amount of transmission and exchange of knowledge thanks to ongoing collaboration with Chinese architects, who have been called on to work with them on high-profile projects. Secondly, a training programme has been set up that allows young Chinese architects to combine their initial studies in China with complementary studies abroad, whether in Europe or in the United States. Finally, there has been the political will to effect a radical alteration of the urban landscape within a series of constraints, initially sociological and economic, and now ecological. This has sometimes been done in response to international events, such as the Olympic Games, and it has given the world of architecture a scope of action of unprecedented temporal and spatial dimensions.

Most visionaries and futurologists had foreseen this sudden catch-up, but in reality the majority of their predictions have been largely surpassed.

Creating an authentic architectural style in such a context gives rise to diverse strategies, and this allows for the expression of strong individual personalities. In the space of fifteen years, architects and urban planners have incorporated the rise of non-State promoters and double-digit growth, but also, and more recently, the tribulations of pollution, responses to sustainable development and reflections on Chinese cultural heritage.

With Fang Zhenning, the broad selection of architects and artists has left only limited room for foreign architects practising in China. These foreigners are the only ones, to our minds, who have played crucial roles and have had substantial influence on the new generation of Chinese architects during this brief transition period. This is not to pass judgement on the quality of the many buildings executed by other Western architects, which have also become landmarks in contemporary world architecture.

The diversity of programmes shown by the selected projects bears witness to the remarkable capacity of adaptation on the part of the Chinese teams. Although they address head-on the question of scale – which, even more than in other contexts, is a critical factor in architecture and urban planning – these projects cannot be reduced to that alone. There is no doubt that a concern for detail drives architects such as Wang Shu, a recent winner of the Global Award for Sustainable Architecture, in which CIVA has played an active role. We think it essential to accord him pride of place, above all for his personal commitment to sustainable architecture, which is invigorated by an ongoing concern for the aesthetic derived from traditional architectural materials. Other architects also make use of ancestral architectural expressions, which they transform into contemporary architectural language. The *tulou* model, or the incorporation of Beijing *hutongs* into interior courtyards, is part of this process.

The selection highlights the emergence of a Chinese architectural identity rather than a specific Chinese architecture separated off from major contemporary movements. This is not just a semantic distinction, but rather the difficult expression of a universal problem among the major architectural issues of our times. China is in no way separate from the rest of the world.

Indeed, these urban developments underscore an indissoluble link between a certain typically Chinese conception of public space and the construction of buildings in this space. They also highlight an age-old preoccupation with a landscape in which the garden and nature are an integrated part of a whole, dedicated to human activities.

The process of overcoming these conflicts and paradoxes in order to reach a sense of harmony finds concrete expression in a number of the projects presented. This kind of ambition is an intimate part of Chinese culture.

The architects and Fang Zhenning himself were able to give their thoughts on their projects and thus provide us with an insider's perspective. These personal commentaries are presented in their own words.

The exhibition, as well as this publication, marks a turning point in the history of Chinese architecture. A close collaboration between China and Belgium has allowed for a dialogue between European and Chinese ways of looking at architecture. Fang Zhenning, through his extensive cataloguing and profound knowledge of the Chinese art scene, has helped us to avoid the often-insurmountable stumbling block of relative Eurocentrism. This seems to us to be the cornerstone in constructing a dialogue refocused on what might be called 'the avant-garde of Chinese architecture'.

Christophe Pourtois has been director of the Centre International pour la Ville, l'Architecture et le Paysage (CIVA) since it was created in 1999. He is an official of the Court of Audit of Belgium. He graduated in Law and Tax Law at the Université Libre de Bruxelles and in History of Art and Architecture at the Université Lille 3 – Charles de Gaulle. In addition to his role as director, he has organized exhibitions at the CIVA and elsewhere, including the V&A in London and the Musée des Beaux-Arts in Cherbourg. He is an author, who has contributed to several publications on different subjects connected with contemporary architecture, and is a doctoral student of the Université Libre de Bruxelles.

Marcelle Rabinowicz is an architect and independent curator. She has been working with the CIVA since its creation ten years ago. She is responsible for its exhibitions, including their coordination and production. She has also produced several publications for the CIVA including catalogues, architectural guides and monographs. The exhibitions Marcelle has organized have taken place in Brussels and other venues in Belgium as well as in various other countries. Marcelle is also a tenured Professor at the Université Libre de Bruxelles in the Department of Drawing of the Architecture Faculty 'La Cambre Horta'.

The Power of the Era
A CRITIQUE FROM AN ARCHITECTURAL COMMENTATOR

FANG ZHENNING

We are delighted to be invited by europalia.china 2009 to present the exhibition *Heart-Made The Cutting-Edge of Chinese Contemporary Architecture* in Brussels, the heart of the European Union. We especially thank the International Centre for Urbanism, Architecture and Landscape (CIVA) who have so generously provided the venue and who have worked closely with us on this project, including the superb catalogue published to accompany the exhibition.

Rationale
At a time when China is increasingly becoming the focus of world attention, Chinese architecture and its associated industries have a pivotal role to play as one of the six pillars of national economic development. China is currently constructing more buildings than any other country. The speed and the immense scale of its architectural development have never before been experienced in the history of urbanization.

This exhibition presents a concise introduction to modern architecture in China through photographs, plans, models, animations and videos as well as installations and sound works. We are taking this opportunity to host two conferences introducing a review of the current situation in Chinese contemporary architecture and the art of architecture in China respectively.

Exhibition Concept
The four themes of the festival europalia.china chosen by the Chinese and Belgian committees – Immortal China, Contemporary China, Colourful China, and China and the Rest of the World – provide a highly appropriate platform for this exhibition of architecture. *Heart-Made The Cutting-Edge of Chinese Contemporary Architecture* belongs in the category 'Contemporary China', although it is also an extension of 'Immortal China'. 'Colourful China' is evident in every one of the works on display, including the achievements in architectural discourse between China and the world. All of the works chosen for the exhibition also fit perfectly with the theme 'China and the Rest of the World'.

The Meaning of 'Heart-Made'
The Chinese characters that mean to 'compose', 'build' or 'construct', are related to human activities of the hand and the heart. Good design comes from the heart and the heart is the centre of morality. Furthermore, architects have a responsibility to act in a moral way.

'Heart-made' can therefore be considered as an updated version of the words to compose, build or construct: to create something from the heart, whether an ideal building or an ideal city. There are two forms of traditional Chinese literature: *tian gong kai wu* and *wen xin diao long*, literally translated as 'products created by nature and technology' and 'dragon-carving [a rhetorical expression meaning literature written or created] by a literal heart'. *Tian gong kai wu* can also be understood as 'products created by enlightenment' and *wen xin diao long* can be elaborated as 'to create by heart'.

'Heart-made' emphasizes the concept of harmony between humankind and nature. The power of design comes from the heart, but it must be compatible with the power of nature – only then are we able to build a good building or city. A permanent building or a city can be described as a continuation of what I mean by this. We decided to take 'heart-made' as the main theme of the exhibition *The Cutting-Edge of Chinese Contemporary Architecture* in order to demonstrate our moral stance towards the process of a permanent development in Chinese architecture and design.

Exhibition
The exhibition is divided into four main topics. 'Live Architecture' includes projects that are recently finished or still in process. 'Digital Architecture' presents the work of digital designers whose designs anticipate the way cities may look and function in the future. These first two topics constitute the main body of this exhibition. 'Video Architecture' includes the work of artists and architects who have observed buildings or cities in their films and animations. 'Sound Art' is also covered in the exhibition. We hope that we will thus be able to present the multi-faceted and diverse nature of our cities.

The main aim of this exhibition can be understood from the identities of its participants. The architects, property developers, educators, video artists and sound artists of our cities are the main players and among them architects and artists stand on the revolutionary frontier of contemporary Chinese architecture.

Displayed in this exhibition are the most representative projects of their kind, including schools, art galleries, apartments for low-income communities, kindergartens, information centres, churches, office buildings, renovated residential courtyards, townscapes, construction sites and the art of sound in the cities. There are also short films about each participant in the exhibition.

Options

The issue of sustainable development in architecture and everyday life in China has drawn worldwide attention, well beyond the heightened interest in China during the Olympics.

Our intention with the construction projects selected for this exhibition has not specifically been to attract the eye, nor have we included those new Chinese landmarks that are already well known in the Western world. The purpose of this exhibition is to help visitors gain a better understanding of the paradigm shift in Chinese architectural trends via visual images from the last ten years.

It is not easy to select only a limited number of architects and a limited number of projects to represent the current state of contemporary architecture in China, since it is such a big country with extensive territories. Some people might ask why Rem Koolhaas and Steven Holl came to be selected rather than other talented foreign architects who are also positively involved in construction projects in China. The reason we chose Koolhaas was not because of his eye-catching designs in China, but because of the radical changes in design and the ideas he contributed to architectural life in China after 2002. The collaborative nature of Holl's working relations with his Chinese partners makes his influence all the greater in Chinese architecture. On the other hand, no other property developer has so successfully improved the cultural aspects of business architecture or given such impetus to governmental property development – which, incidentally, is largely being driven by private property developers – than the SOHO China's CEO, Pan Shiyi.

The most important aspect of this exhibition is to introduce specific Chinese architects and their backgrounds and achievements. Half of the architects represented here studied architecture overseas before coming back to China, while the other half graduated from domestic universities. The fact that the numbers of returning students majoring in architecture and those of architects from domestic universities represented in this exhibition are equal is entirely accidental. All of them are pillars of our society. But we also had the opportunity to invite the younger generation of architects who were born after 1980 to participate in this exhibition. Their designs and ideas provide an insight into future developments in architecture for China.

There could be many more alternative designs from such a big world stage for architecture. In this case, the selection criterion has been determined by 'heart-made' – the theme of this exhibition. The formal-istic design may interfere with our capacity to make an objective value judgement, therefore it was crucial to formulate criteria for our decisions. We benefited from our confidence on this point, because it enabled us to see and understand the motivations of designers in order to make a judgement about the worthiness of their endeavours in society.

The Meaning of Contemporary

What do we mean by contemporary? The word is often used when referring to adolescence and covers everything that is full of youth-ful vigour. What we call contemporary architecture can broadly be understood as architectural designs in their period of adolescence, against which no other power can compete. Such is the power of our contemporary times.

Any human activity related to design that does not have any artistic aspiration is monotonous; the same goes for exhibitions about urban architecture. This attempt to present the multiple dimensions of the Chinese city provides us with the opportunity to hold a party for everyone, including our participating artists and architects.

10 April 2009, Beijing

Fang Zhenning is a well-known Chinese architecture and art critic and independent curator. He regularly reviews art and architecture using a wide range of influences. As a consultant in China Central Television (CCTV) and senior writer of 'ABITARE', he has written millions of words in critical essays. Fang is also a blogger who has gained a tremendous number of readers with his incisive views. Finally, he is the director of Fang Media Studio and a visiting professor in his graduate school, China Central Academy of Fine Arts. Fang lives in Beijing.

ARCHITECTURAL TRENDS

PAN Shiyi

ZAHA Hadid Architects

KOOLHAAS Rem / OMA (Office for Metropolitan Architecture)

PAN Shiyi / SOHO China: Cities in Transition

In the expansive reception area at SOHO China's head office, located in Chaowai SOHO in Beijing's Central Business District (CBD), historical photographs hang on the walls. The pictures show the former location of Beijing's No. 1 Machinery Factory, its buildings, the demolition of the factory's main workshop in June 2001, the construction of the Jianwai SOHO and the grand celebrations following its completion. These pictures are so representative that they could almost be regarded as the epitome of how Chinese cities are being transformed in the twenty-first century.

Among the many Chinese property developers, the private company SOHO China has instigated a number of distinctive architectural styles and plays a leading role in the process of promoting the urbanization of China. SOHO New Town was the first large-scale architectural project undertaken by SOHO China in the late 1990s. Its façade does not seem so fashionable now, but at the time it influenced several impressive architectural complexes, including the Huamao Centre, Wanda Square and the Jindi Centre.

SOHO China's most successful project is undoubtedly the Jianwai SOHO, located to the east of Chang'an Avenue, Beijing's most famous street, and to the south of the China World Trade Centre. Designed by the Japanese architect Riken Yamamoto, this architectural project is the largest new complex in Beijing's CBD District so far. It includes eighteen commercial and residential apartment blocks, two office buildings, four villas and a plethora of retail outlets. There is a full range of facilities, including kindergartens, clubs and the CBD's biggest central greenbelt. Each day, around one hundred thousand people work, shop and enjoy themselves here, but on its completion, only a few people saw its full potential. Nowadays, with sixteen pedestrian streets, three hundred stores and twenty rooftop gardens, the community has already proved itself superior not only to similar projects in the CBD District and elsewhere in Beijing, but also to all the other projects by SOHO China itself. Toyo Ito, the famous Japanese architect, has praised Jianwai SOHO, stating: 'This is the largest complete minimalist architectural complex I have ever seen in the world.'

While many people make up the community of Jianwai SOHO, few are aware of its history. The site is the former location of Beijing's No. 1 Machinery Factory, the largest machine manufacturer in China for the past fifty years, which was once a great symbol of China's industry. When the factory was demolished in June 2001, its destruction came to symbolize the new urbanization of Beijing. And when the first group of white lattice towers was constructed to the south of Chang'an Avenue, their whiteness lit up Beijing.

In the lead-up to the 2008 Olympic Games, the city of Beijing looked like a huge construction site, with countless private development projects underway. It seemed to be compensating for the previously unresolved problems of supply and demand in commercial and residential accommodation, which it had endured for half a century. The construction of Jianwai SOHO has introduced a new high-quality urban environment that has had a real impact on people's lives. Rather than simply changing the shape of existing communities, it has reformed the old way of living in Beijing, which had prevailed for hundreds of years.

Beijing is an old city which was founded more than six hundred years ago. Traditionally, its residents lived in a type of courtyard structure known as a *siheyuan*, ensuring an extremely private family lifestyle. Breaking down the walls of the city or the courtyard is the first step towards urban modernization. A number of more open residential and educational structures, including some intended for government offices and the military, had in fact already been built in Beijing during the 1950s, but these still included walls and railings to separate people.

Jianwai SOHO introduced the most recent transformation of the construction layout. The walls dividing the community have disappeared, turning the streets into communal spaces. Small squares and gardens in random sizes, with facilities for pedestrians to rest and relax, are provided throughout the streets and public spaces. The sunken courtyard spaces were inspired by the cave-dwellings of northern China, the first time the idea had been incorporated into such a large-scale design. The architect diverted the roads underground to separate the traffic from the pedestrians. Some commercial spaces are also located at the lower levels, making the whole area multi-layered. Moreover, if one sets north, south, east and west as the axes, each building is rotated at an angle of 45 degrees. This layout allows all four elevations of each building to receive sunshine, while avoiding poor views and ensuring privacy. The unified, abstract appearance of Jianwai SOHO's façades and towers create a sharp contrast with the multifarious structures all around, forming a unique landscape in Beijing.

When it was first completed, people were eager to know more about the developers and architects of Jianwai SOHO. As time passes, Jianwai SOHO has become a successful and fashionable area of Beijing. Initially it seemed like an explosion of froth, a product of ambitious developers and architects caught up in Beijing's rapid development. Now, the seas have grown calmer. Perhaps the project has already achieved the original aspirations of its architects, that of making the architecture the environment itself, as an organic element of the city.

JIANWAI SOHO

LOCATION: **39 Dongsanhuan Zhonglu Road, Chaoyang District, Beijing, China**
ARCHITECT: **Riken Yamamoto**
PROJECT TEAM: **Riken Yamamoto & Field Shop, Japan, SAKO Architects**
CONSTRUCTION PERIOD: **2002–2007**
SITE AREA: **169,000 m²**
BUILDING AREA: **683,821 m²**
DEVELOPER: **SOHO China Ltd.**
USE: **housing, offices, retail**

P15
Riken Yamamoto turned his concept of
a 'cell city', which he came up with 10 years
ago, into reality at Jianwai SOHO on Chang'
an Avenue in Beijing
© SOHO China

P17
The sensational opening ceremony of
Jianwai SOHO, 25 April 2004
© SOHO China

P18-P19
1. Beijing's No. 1 Machinery Factory was once a
   great symbol of China's industry
   © SOHO China
2. The main workshop of Beijing's No. 1
   Machinery Factory was demolished in June
   2001
   © SOHO China
3. The white architectural complex has become
   the focal point of Beijing's Central Business
   District (CBD)
   © SOHO China
4. Each building at Jianwai SOHO rotates 45
   degrees eastwards from the north–south
   axes and is located on different lines
   © SOHO China
5. Jianwai SOHO at night
   © SOHO China
6. Jianwai SOHO at night
   © SOHO China

1

2

3

4

5

6

CHAOYANGMEN SOHO (PHASE III)

LOCATION: **Chao Yang Men, Beijing, China**
ARCHITECT: **Zaha Hadid Architects**
DESIGN TEAM: **Satoshi Ohashi, Raymond Lau**
CONSTRUCTION PERIOD: **2009–2012**
SITE AREA: **over 50,000 m²**
BUILDING AREA: **334,000 m²**
USE: **offices and shopping centre**

DESCRIPTION Chaoyangmen SOHO (Phase III) is the latest project in Beijing developed by SOHO China. It is designed by the world famous architect Zaha Hadid who collaborated with SOHO China in 2003. Inspired by the Chinese theme of the courtyard, the project creates an internal world of retail and offices which is located in a desirable part of Beijing beside the East Second Ring Road. The design concept of the project involves four individual volumes which coalesce and fuse into a spectacular whole. The elastic shapes of the corridors and stretch bridges blend individual volumes, forming the main circulation routes which connect each of the atriums, creating dynamic continuity of interior spaces and outdoor terraces. The project contains a linear park in the front, green spaces all around and great interior courtyards. It is the most futuristic project by SOHO China since Jianwai SOHO.

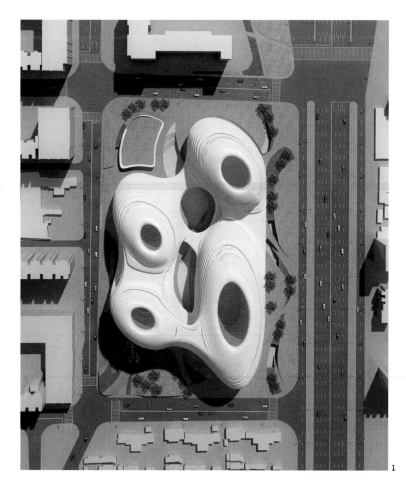

KOOLHAAS Rem / OMA (Office for Metropolitan Architecture): Thoughts on Design and Architecture

The opening up of Beijing to the world of international architectural design should have begun in April 1998, after the French architect Paul Andreu won the bid to design the National Grand Theatre. But his victory failed to ignite any bright sparks of creativity in the Chinese architectural world. Instead, Andreu's project started a wave of controversy that continued until its completion ten years later. For China, a country with a long architectural tradition, the construction of such a large-scale building in so important an area by a foreigner was unprecedented.

The Chinese architectural design world certainly took notice, however, when the Dutch architect Rem Koolhaas, founder of the Netherlands Office for Metropolitan Architecture (OMA), won the contest to design the China Central Television (CCTV) building in October 2002. Due to the significance of the victory by Koolhaas and Ole Scheeren's team, I immediately posted a blog on a well-known Chinese architectural design website of the time, with the title: 'Koolhaas – turning a new page in Chinese architectural history.' Before my post, the Chinese media knew nothing about Koolhaas. After his victory, the architect rapidly became a major focus of media attention.

The first country fully to embrace Koolhaas's ideas in Asia was Japan. In 1995, Tokyo hosted a citywide event entitled, 'Rem Koolhaas and the Place of Public Architecture', which escalated Koolhaas's popularity. The following October, the famed architect hosted a series of workshops in the Japanese city. Taking 'Asia: Redefining the City' as his theme, Koolhaas declared his vision for Asia's future. He predicted that 'by the year 2020, 17% of the world's markets and two-thirds of the world's megacities will all be in Asia'. Koolhaas was one of the first architectural thinkers to pay attention to the development of Asia's cities. During the workshop, I wrote a report entitled, 'Rem Koolhaas cyclones to Asia'. This was the first time Koolhaas's name had appeared in the Chinese media. Thirteen years later, the reality of Asia's development has verified Koolhaas's predictions.

Why did I say Koolhaas 'turned a new page in Chinese architecture'? We have to consider the situation at that time in Beijing. After China's successful Olympic bid, there was a rush to construct large-scale public buildings and an urgent need to develop Beijing's CBD (Central Business District) using world-class construction techniques and designs. However, at the time, there was an insufficient understanding of modern world architecture and a shortage of skilled architects to tackle the work. The proposed design for the CCTV building came about as a direct result of the Chinese edition of a book written by Japanese journalist Masayuki Fuchigami, entitled *World Architects: Concepts and Works*. The recommendations of more than fifty internationally

renowned architects in the book are reflected in the CCTV building's design. This illustrates both the importance of diffusing information and how a single introduction can bring about revolutionary changes and perhaps even trigger a new movement in the field of architecture.

After Koolhaas's successful CCTV bid, he was appointed as a judge in the bidding competition for the design of the National Stadium. Koolhaas awarded bonus points to the 'Bird's Nest' design upon review and final assessment. Olympic buildings and projects all had to fulfil strict standards.

Koolhaas's CCTV building design initially received mixed feedback from the Chinese public. Many were concerned about its aesthetic appearance and the construction costs of the 'loop' shape. However, a few examined the design closely from a functional point of view and praised its flexibility. Domestically produced materials were used to construct the steel framework and walls. OMA also put a great deal of effort into working and cooperating with Chinese manufacturers. Subsequently, these factories were able to learn and incorporate international technologies into their methods, allowing their techniques to meet international standards. Even more important than the simple application of new technologies and materials, however, was how successfully to build the challenging architectural structure.

The general public was concerned that the strange shape of the CCTV building would be difficult to construct. In fact, rather than the construction, the most difficult part of the project was coordinating the design teams. Only those present fully understood the hardships faced by the technical team, which was made up of hundreds of people from five countries who spoke different languages, all trying to reach a consensus and to coordinate their overall ideas. Obviously, there were some challenges in the construction of the CCTV building, the greatest of which was how to solve the docking problem of the different sections forming the structure. These consisted of the leg-like pillars, which were both 161 metres long from top to bottom, and the north–south and east–west sections, which were 68 metres and 74 metres long, respectively.

The project manager of the OMA team, Dongmei Yao, seven years after her first media interview, disclosed some details of the project. 'What astonishes people is the building's appeal,' she said. 'It enabled everyone on the design and construction teams to put their best work and effort into its construction because they each had a great part to play in the building's creation, which filled them with excitement. The building had a kind of attraction, ensuring that everyone involved in the project worked hard to realize its completion. This is precisely what critics are unable to understand; it has a charming design with a powerful appeal, which brought the builders together and struck a responsive chord in their hearts.'

At the time of writing, the CCTV building is nearing completion. The technological sophistication and unprecedented difficulties in the construction of the building will only become evident after its completion. Only then will we finally understand its true significance. The CCTV building will be Beijing's landmark, but it will also be a marker in the world of architecture.

I agree with Yao's point of view on the necessity for high-rise buildings. Yao believes that 'skyscrapers ... can provide a modern urban city with a bird's-eye view of the awakening of a great consciousness kindled in human beings. Through this process, architecture is not only put on display for people to see, it is also intended to arouse people's enthusiasm towards modern urban life; furthermore, it awakens their confidence and aspirations in the collective power of unity. This is what architecture offers people, a different state of mind and of perception.'

Despite mixed reviews, the CCTV building's mystical, striking and futuristic form will stand tall over Beijing. With the passage of time, the people working, living and co-existing with it will eventually grow proud of the massive structure. Great architecture is an art that surpasses time; the CCTV building has paved the way for the development of a modern architectural style in China.

P25
CCTV under construction (2008)
© Fang Zhenning

CCTV

LOCATION: **Central Business District (CBD), Beijing, China**
ARCHITECTS: **Rem Koolhaas, Ole Scheeren (OMA)**
PROJECT TEAM: **Charles Berman, David Chacon, Chris van Duijn, Erez Ella, Adrianne Fisher, Anu Leinonen, André Schmidt, Shohei Shigematsu, Hiromasa Shirai, Steven Smit**
CONSTRUCTION PERIOD: **2004–**
SITE AREA: **465,000 m²**
CLIENT: **China Central Television**

DESCRIPTION The new headquarters for China Central Television, OMA's largest project to date, combines the entire process of making television – administration, production, broadcasting – into a single loop of interconnected activity. Rising from a common platform accommodating the production facilities, two towers – one dedicated to broadcasting, the other to services, research and education – lean towards each other and eventually merge in a dramatic, seemingly impossible, cantilever.

CCTV's distinctive loop aims to offer an alternative to the exhausted typology of the skyscraper. In spite of their potential to incubate new cultures, programmes and ways of life, most skyscrapers accommodate merely routine activity, arranged according to predictable patterns. Formally, their expressions of verticality have tended to stunt the imagination: as verticality soars, creativity crashes.

P26–P27
1. CCTV prototype model
© OMA
2. CCTV under construction (2008)
© Fang Zhenning
3. CCTV under construction (2008)
© Fang Zhenning
4. CCTV main building under construction (2008)
© Fang Zhenning
5. Top floor of the CCTV main building under construction (2008)
© Fang Zhenning

P28–P29
1. The majestic appearance of the CCTV main building, viewed from the TVCC (Television Cultural Centre) building (2008)
© Fang Zhenning
2. The CCTV main building complete with glass curtain walls, viewed from the west (2009)
© Fang Zhenning

4

5

TAIPEI PERFORMING ARTS CENTRE

LOCATION: **Taipei, China**
ARCHITECTS: **Rem Koolhaas, Ole Scheeren (OMA)**
PROJECT TEAM: **André Schmidt, Mariano Sagasta, Adam Frampton**
CONSTRUCTION PERIOD: **2009–2014**
SITE AREA: **40,000 m²**
CLIENT: **Taipei Municipal Government**

DESCRIPTION The ambition of this project is to create three independent theatres – precisely, efficiently and economically – in a design that offers urban intensification and unexpected theatrical possibilities as additional benefits.

Over several visits, we have been able to experience the vitality of the theatre in Taipei. Surprisingly to the foreign visitor, the public includes all generations, young and old and, seemingly, all classes.

Theatre directors are cult heroes in Taipei. It seems as if Taiwan's own history, with its drastic political divisions and constant upheavals, has provided a fertile breeding ground, as though its tensions and traumas can best be presented and resolved on stage.

Our theatre is not a token sign of culture but a sophisticated tool equal to the ambition of Taiwan's theatre-makers.

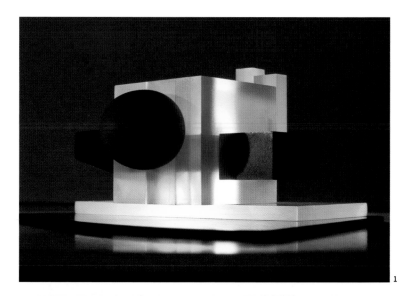

1

2

Combinations

Combining the three stages and technical apparatus of the three theatres in a single apparatus, we have generated not only three functional, perfectly independent theatres that operate with complete autonomy, we have also incorporated additional potentials – both vertically and horizontally – that create unsuspected further scenarios and uses. The Design offers the advantages of specificity with the freedoms of the undefined.

The cube is bisected by two axes, one horizontal – the Grand Theatre and Multiform Theatre at either end – and one vertical, extending from the Proscenium Playhouse downward to the an open stage for Puppet Theatre.

As they intersect, they guarantee both smooth, autonomous functioning of each individual hall and extreme flexibility for alternative uses.

3

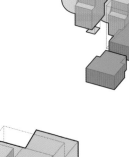

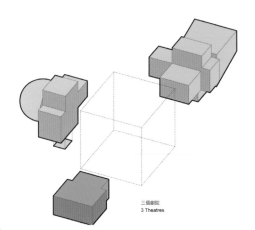

三個劇院
3 Theatres

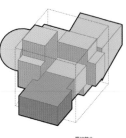

壓縮整合
Compression

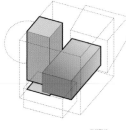

交錯聯接
Cross Connection

P30–P31
1. Conceptual prototype model
© OMA
2. Artist's impression of the Taipei Performing Arts Centre at night
© OMA
3. Conceptual diagrams for the Taipei Performing Arts Centre
© OMA
4. Prototype model
© OMA
5. Prototype model
© OMA

30

4

5

SHENZHEN CRYSTAL ISLAND

LOCATION: **Shenzhen, China**
ARCHITECTS: **Ole Scheeren (OMA) and Meng Yan (Urbanus)**
PROJECT TEAM: **OMA and Urbanus**
CONSTRUCTION PERIOD: **2009**
SITE AREA: **450,000 m²**

DESCRIPTION The Office for Metropolitan Architecture (OMA), in collaboration with Urbanus Architecture & Design Inc., have been awarded the first prize in the design competition for Shenzhen's new civic centre, underground interchange and public landmark. An international jury selected the design, led by OMA partner Ole Scheeren, from thirty-two entries.

The scheme builds on Shenzhen's newly acquired status of 'City of Design', awarded by UNESCO in 2008, and proposes the formation of a Shenzhen Creative Centre, a complex for the city's creative industries adjacent to the city hall.

Two systems are superimposed to form the nexus of Shenzhen Creative Centre – an underground system of 'shortcut connectors' linking existing and future train and Metro stations to create a central transport hub; and a creative landscape with 'design villages' and clusters of activity above ground that are linked by an elevated pedestrian walkway. At the heart of the two systems is the 'Shenzhen Eye', a spherical void that will become Shenzhen's new landmark: a symbolic 'space of the imagination'.

An expansive 20-hectare landscape of parks and gardens, populated by clusters of pavilions and activities, and connected by pedestrian infrastructure, creates a vibrant micro-urbanism in the heart of the city. Its scale is large, but the elements are small and in proportion with its natural surroundings and the human beings that inhabit them. It is an urban playground with a multiplicity of condensed and flexible ad-hoc conditions – truly a creative landscape.

The Shenzhen Creative Centre introduces a space that fosters urbanism without density, supports aggregation through interconnected activities and creates a focal point for Shenzhen, 'City of Design'. Previously dispersed creative industries will be linked by means of an integrated infrastructure and cultivated in a landscape of multiplicity, transparency and openness towards creative activity.

The collaboration of OMA and Urbanus included Ole Scheeren, Rem Koolhaas and Urbanus partner Meng Yan, together with a team led by OMA associates Dongmei Yao and Anu Leinonen.

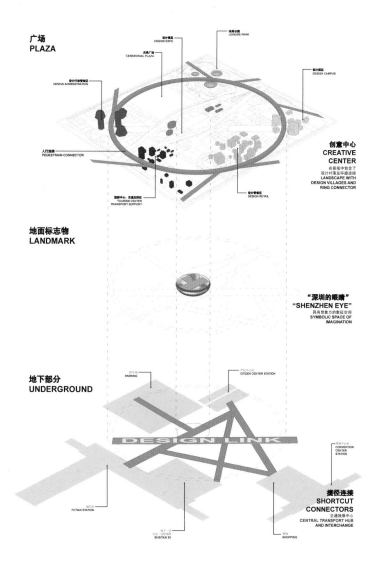

P32-P33
1. Conceptual drawing
© OMA / Ole Scheeren
2. View of Shenzhen Crystal Island at night
© OMA / Ole Scheeren

P34-P35
1. View of Shenzhen Crystal Island by day
© OMA / Ole Scheeren
2. View of Shenzhen Crystal Island at night
© OMA / Ole Scheeren
3. Model
© OMA/ Ole Scheeren

LIVE ARCHITECTURE

CUI Kai

HOU Liang

HU Yue

LI Xinggang

LIANG Jingyu

LIU Jiakun

LÜ Pinjing

MA Yansong / MAD

URBANUS

WANG Shu

WANG Yun

WANG Dengyue

ZHU Pei / WU Tong

ZHUANG Weimin

HOLL Steven / LI Hu

The Rising Chinese Architects

The arrival of European and American architects and firms into the Chinese architectural arena is the result of China's thirty-year process of reform and opening up and has occurred, for the most part, over the past decade. China's architectural market has presented the world with an unprecedented degree of openness – and has been the subject of spirited domestic debate, with the conservative viewpoint alleging that China has become a testing ground for foreign architects. Controversy on this point is quite common in the media, although it is becoming less fierce.

In point of fact, every fast-growing city throughout history has served as a testing ground for the world's architects to show off their ability, though the appearance of this phenomenon in China has a greater meaning. China lacks a modernist architecture movement and individual architectural firms have emerged only over the past decade or so. With such a recent starting point for Chinese architecture, few have been optimistic in their predictions about when Chinese architects are likely to catch up with their international counterparts. The current realities of Chinese architecture, however, provide unprecedented opportunities for Chinese architects. Nobody would have anticipated that even as China 'imports' architecture and design, Chinese architects have also begun to 'export' their own designs overseas. This is inextricably tied to the greater story of the rise of China overall. The 'Chinese century' will bring new wonders to world architecture – but it should be noted that many Chinese architects still lack a distinctive style.

The neighbouring country of Japan provides a useful comparison. Japan was the first Asian country to experiment successfully at home with the modernism it had learned overseas, but it still took nearly half a century to progress from 'importing' foreign architects to 'exporting' its architecture overseas. China, by comparison, has moved from the one to the other in only a decade or so – a 'great leap forward' indeed.

In 2005, Zhang Yonghe, Director of Peking University's Graduate School of Architecture left to become Dean of the Massachusetts Institute of Technology's architecture school – the first ethnically Chinese scholar to lead a major architecture department in America. In 2006, Ma Qingyun was named Dean of the University of Southern California's School of Architecture – possibly the first time the position had been held by a foreign national. As in the area of education, Chinese architects have also made great strides forward in design. In 2006, the Chinese architect Ma Yansong won an international competition in Canada – the first Chinese architect to do so – and in early 2007, Zhu Pei was invited by the Guggenheim Foundation to design a pavilion in Abu Dhabi for the proposed Saadiyat Island Cultural District scheme.

There is, however, still a long way for Chinese architects to go before their works can be regarded as classics of world architecture. To start with, individual Chinese architects have yet to develop a distinct, recognizable style. In addition, China has yet to produce architectural works that truly impress on an emotional level. The rise of China has the potential to bring new lights and new talents to the world of architecture. But even as nearly all of the world's architecture magazines publish special editions about Chinese architecture, architectural publishing houses release volumes containing works by Chinese architects and leading architectural journals release Chinese-language editions – as though without China they would become less contemporary – we know very well that even if there is a brief fashion for Chinese architecture, flooding the world with Chinese architects lacking individual style would serve only to lower global architectural standards.

The achievements of China's leading architects are, of course, tied to the overall rise of China – but their genius, and their success, lie in their choice of venue for their talent, their decision to hitch their stars to the 'China Express'. Architecture is a difficult business anywhere, but especially so in China, where rules and regulations in almost every area have yet to be refined. What China's leading architects bring to the table internationally, therefore, is their years of experience and courage in the areas of communications, education, design and urban planning.

The unprecedented speed and scale of construction in China has made the country a stage for world architecture. The seven years following China's winning bid for the 2008 Olympic Games was a period in which Chinese architects became increasingly influenced by Western fashions and it came with an unprecedented period of reaction and reflection. While it might appear at a glance that all of the major Olympic projects were won by foreign architects or firms, the cooperation and partnership of Chinese architectural groups led to a corresponding leap forward in China's own design ability and capacity for cooperation.

China's period of intensive construction has provided for many a level playing field for design and competition. Fresh, idealistic young Chinese architects have used this era to display their own skills and to grow and mature quickly in a more cosmopolitan environment. They are the mainstay of the Chinese architecture world today. We should be thankful to live in such an age, for it will become the backdrop to the rise of the Chinese architect.

CUI Kai: The Essence of Tibet

In 1982, Cui Kai, who showed great talent from a very early age, won first prize for his 'Architect's House' design from the National Architecture Students design competition. Although he has been Director of the Chinese Architecture Design and Research Institute for many years, his heart and focus remain set on design. He has presided over and initiated the design of more than fifty projects, including hotels, museums, gymnasiums, libraries, office buildings, universities, railway stations, embassies, science and technology centres, administrative buildings and garden villas. The most experienced architect among his peers, this pillar of the architectural industry was born and raised in China, where, over the past twenty years, he has established an incomparable architectural legacy.

Lhasa Railway Station, built between 2004 and 2006, was no mere structural feat. The extreme effort he put into its construction and the project's significance has made it one of his most powerful works to date. The attributes and style of the building make it Tibetan in nature. On the one hand, it is a sapiential gift, a work of wisdom; while, on the other hand, the work possesses a strong regionalism, a form of Tibetan architecture that is at the service of the Tibetan people.

Lhasa Railway Station is the final stop of the Qinghai–Tibet line, a route of 1,956 kilometres, starting at Xining City in Qing Hai Province and ending in Lhasa, the capital of the Tibet Autonomous Region. The 814-kilometre section from Xining to Golmud was completed in 1984, followed by the 1,142-kilometre section from Golmud to Lhasa in 2006. At an average altitude of 3,700 metres above sea level, the climate in Lhasa is arid with strong sunlight. Such challenging natural conditions make any problems of design and construction seem almost irrelevant by comparison. As well as considering the station's public spaces, the designers also took into account its upper sections. The roof is fitted with solar panels, harnessing the sun's energy to warm the interior of the station via underfloor heating. To ventilate such a large building and avoid the need to open and close the lofty upper windows, special ventilation shafts were adopted to keep out the dust. Even during the spring and autumn dust storms the air inside the station remains clean.

The station's design gave architects the opportunity to learn from Tibetan architecture, which is characterized by its use of topography, in which architecture and landscape are melded into one: a perfect example being the Potala Palace. The railway station is located in a vast open space to the south of a valley, backed by mountains and with a river to the front. In order to best use the available space, the architects took advantage of the length of platforms to design a building extending horizontally. Work on both projects took a year and half to complete and was carried out under low-oxygen conditions.

P38-P39
1. Red and white concrete panels were used inside the station
   © Zhang Guangyuan
2. The design of the main entrance incorporates many regional features
   © Zhang Guangyuan

LHASA RAILWAY STATION

LOCATION: **Liuwu New District, Lhasa, Tibet Autonomous Region**
ARCHITECT: **Cui Kai**
PROJECT TEAM: **Shan Lixin, Zhao Xiaogang, Zheng Meng**
CONSTRUCTION PERIOD: **2004–2006**
SITE AREA: **111,646 m²**
BUILDING AREA: **23,697 m²**

P40–P41
1. Solar roof panels
   © Zhao Xiaogang
2. Lhasa Railway Station beneath the clear
   skies of the Tibetan Plateau
   © Zhang Guangyuan

DESCRIPTION The 1,956-kilometre Qinghai–Tibet railway line starts in Xining, Qinghai Province and ends at Lhasa, the capital of Tibet. The 814-kilometre Xining to Germ section was opened in 1984 and the construction of the 1,142-kilometre Germ to Lhasa section was completed in 2006. This is the highest and longest plateau railway line in the world. Lhasa Railway Station is the terminus of the Qinghai to Tibet railway line.

Lhasa Station is located in the south-west of the city, in the Liuwu New District on the south bank of the Lhasa River, 2 kilometres from the city centre. From here, you can just see the Potala Palace in the distance and the famous Zhaibung Temple on the hills across the river. The site topography is flat and open, the elevation changing from high to low as it moves from south to north. The total site area is 111,642 m² and the complex includes the railway station, railway company headquarters, front plaza and streets leading to the station. According to the development plan, Lhasa Station will initially host five pairs of non-stop trains, later increasing to six pairs of trains. The whole station has an open-plan layout with one main platform, three intermediate platforms and seven railway lines. The 500-metre platform is covered entirely by a suspended roof with no supporting columns. The station is located to the north of the railway lines. It has a total floor area of 23,697 m² and a maximum capacity of 2,000 people.

Lhasa is situated on the Tibetan Plateau at an average altitude of 3,700 metres above sea level. The air oxygen content is only 70% of that in the plain area. It has an average annual air temperature of 7.8 °C, with a maximum of 29.6 °C and a minimum of -16.5 °C. Average annual rainfall is 406.8 mm, with an average annual evaporation of 1975.7 mm. It is relatively dry with very strong sunlight. In such a unique climate, the design needs to be appropriately adapted – the founding principle of architecture with vernacular features. For example, to minimize the walking distance for visitors the road leads right up to the entrance hall. Similarly, the shallow depth of building allows easy access to the platforms. To shade the interior from sunlight, the external windows are long and narrow. They are also densely divided and stepped back into the tapered walls, achieving a more shaded effect. At the same time, multiple solar energy panels on the roof take advantage of the sunlight – the solar energy produced heats the water used for underfloor heating. As for natural ventilation, the highest windows are often hard to open in such tall architectural spaces, so dust-proofing ventilation troughs were designed and placed beneath the windows, allowing clean air to enter the room even during the windy days of spring and autumn. The dry climate and wide daily variations in temperature on the Tibetan Plateau can cause cracking in the surface of walls and columns. Following expert advice, prefabricated reinforced concrete external wall panels were selected for their excellent weather resistance and durability.

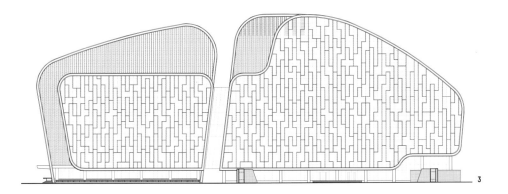

3

BEIJING DIGITAL PRESS INFORMATION CENTRE

LOCATION: **Beijing, China**
ARCHITECTS: **Cui Kai, Zheng Shiwei, He Yongmei, Jing Quan, Lin Zhuo, Lin Lei, Zhou Yu**
CONSTRUCTION PERIOD: **2004–2007**
SITE AREA: **10,454 m²**
BUILDING AREA: **49,000 m²**

DESCRIPTION The old city of Beijing is composed of courtyards with undulating skylines, dignified colours and exquisite details. Could these be reinterpreted to create a new kind of native architectural vocabulary?

The apparent chaos of urban buildings conceals a rigorous relationship between spaces. Well-controlled daylight regulations define the density of Chinese cities. Set on the boundaries of old Beijing city, this building's unusual profile derives from its varying height. Besides the contrasting heights of its north and south sides, the scale of its east and west aspects are also quite different. Constructed between a historic royal palace and the huge CNOOC office building, the site presented the great challenge of how best to find harmony between the scale of the traditional inner city and the rapidly growing modern city. According to the client's demands, the building is divided into two parts, both wrapped with undulating surfaces connecting the variations in height. This satisfies the daylight regulations, maximizes the use of space and echoes both the pitched roofs of the traditional courtyard building and the curved curtain wall of the CNOOC block. The vertical shades on the east and west façades magnify the building's scale, creating a balance with its gigantic neighbour, while the zigzag forms of the shades give a suggestion of a traditional context, linking the building to the traditional courtyard. The curved surface extends into the lobby emphasizing the integrality of the architectural language. The colours, materials and garden-like design also represent a regionalist theme. Telling the story behind the design is not to deny the influence of current trends in fashion, but it explains the rationale behind the design process.

P42-P43
1. View of the curtain wall
   © Zhang Guangyuan
2. The main entrance viewed from Chaowai Street
   © Zhang Guangyuan
3. Sketch plan
   © Cui Kai
4. The Qing Dynasty royal palace to the west
   © Zhang Guangyuan
5. Profile of the Beijing Digital Press Information Centre and roof of the Qing Dynasty royal palace
   © Zhang Guangyuan

4   5

±0.000标高平面图

PEACHBLOSSOM VALLEY VISITOR CENTRE, MOUNT TAI

LOCATION: **Tai'an City, Shandong Province, China**
ARCHITECT: **Cui Kai**
PROJECT TEAM: **Wu Bin**
STRUCTURE: **reinforced concrete shear-wall structure**
CONSTRUCTION PERIOD: **2009–2010**
SITE AREA: **36,259 m²**
BUILDING AREA: **7,685 m²**
USE: **culture and tourism**

DESCRIPTION This project is situated in the Peachblossom Valley, which lies to the west of Mount Tai. The site incorporates two car parks constructed at different levels. To the south is the Nanmatao Reservoir, which is fed by streams from the upper reaches of the Colourstone River. To the east are several villages and an army barracks. The road, which leads to an inn on the far banks of the reservoir, lies to the west of the project.

The public and private parking areas are accessed by a long ramp, facilitating the flow of incoming and outgoing tourists and built to harmonize with the topography of the site. The two access routes cross vertically, allowing for a visual connection without interrupting the flow, a solution that satisfies the fundamental requirements of the tourist centre's management of visitors. Water from the lake is incorporated into the structure, channelled along the ramp to create a focal point.

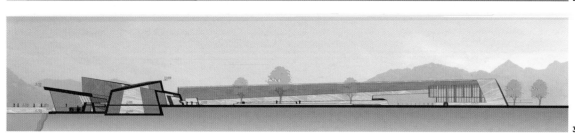

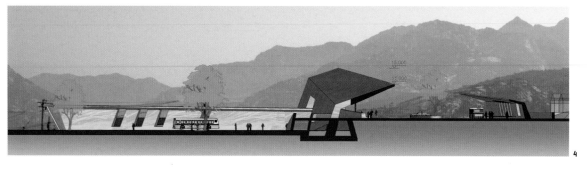

P44-P45
1. ±0.000 site plan
   © Cui Kai Studio
2. The horizontal structure at the foot of Mount Tai
   © Cui Kai Studio
3. Cross-section
   © Cui Kai Studio
4. Cross-section
   © Cui Kai Studio
5. The building has the appearance of a stone carved in two parts, with water flowing through the middle
   © Cui Kai Studio
6. The waiting area
   © Cui Kai Studio
7. The structure, with its defined edges and sharp corners, complements its beautiful surroundings
   © Cui Kai Studio

44

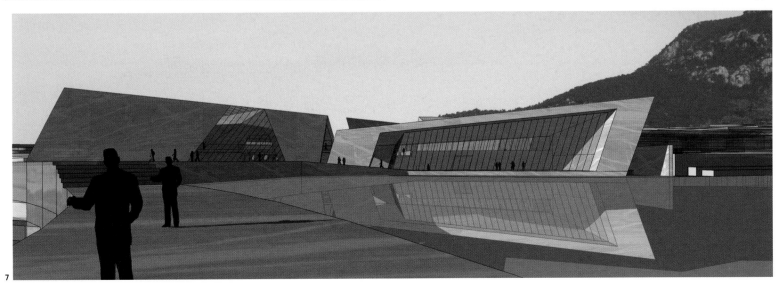

5

6

7

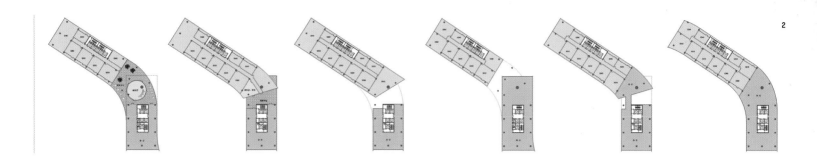

DESCRIPTION Part of the Jiangbei District development in Chongqing, the project lies within the boundaries of the new city – City Of Memories – situated near the historical site of Jinyang Gate. The Jialing River runs to the south of the project, separating the new area of the city from the old Yuzhong District. To the west of the project is the developing CBD (Central Business District), while to the east lies the Chongqing Science and Technology Centre and the Grand Theatre.

As a typical mountain city, all the buildings in Chongqing are situated along the hillside. Because of its perpendicular slant, the structures are at different heights giving the city a picturesque appearance. The roads twist and turn, flickering between the buildings of various heights. Seen from a distance, the huge three-dimensional city is organically organized, like a microcosm of life. This urban spatial characteristic has been applied to the design of this project. The different sections of the construction overlap vertically, while in the centre of the building they branch horizontally in different directions. The irregular shape of the building means that the windows in the two sides of the building's upper section have different views across the city. A number of aerial courtyards have been incorporated into the split openings of the upper levels, allowing the introduction of urban public spaces. The different functional patterns at the two sides of the building are well defined, while the working environments at the upper levels are improved by the formation of a three-dimensional urban space facilitating the continuation of everyday activities.

Originally, different kinds of commercial units were arranged alongside the giant steps ascending the mountain. The long, extended steps with stores located at different heights form a commercial environment that is uniquely characteristic of the mountain city. In this project, along the south–north direction of the building's annexe, a giant curved stairway is designed to connect the main entrances of the different floors, from the first floor to the third floor of the commercial annexe. Solid blocks of planting soften the contours of the giant steps and small commercial franchised stores in picture-frame styles are arranged along the two sides at different heights, creating the sense of a modern commercial space with local characteristics and improving the stores' commercial appeal. Since they are constructed on a slope, the entrances to the commercial spaces are also organized at different heights, maximizing their commercial potential.

JIN YANG MEN, CHONGQING

LOCATION: **Chongqing, China**
ARCHITECT: **Cui Kai**
COLLABORATORS: **Christian Hennecke, Liu Heng, He Lijian, Li Bing**
CONSTRUCTION PERIOD: **2007–**
SITE AREA: **7,568 m²**
BUILDING AREA: **99,938 m²**
USE: **annexe, offices, hotel apartments**

P46-P47

1. Overlapping volumes on the vertical dimension
© Cui Kai Studio

2. Floor plans
© Cui Kai Studio

3. Different building volumes create a three-dimensional urban window with views of the street
© Cui Kai Studio

HOU Liang:
Space Installation – 'Zhuan Xin Ting'

Born in Shanghai, China, Hou Liang graduated from the Katholieke Universiteit Leuven, Belgium, with a master's degree in architecture. In 2003, Hou Liang founded his own design studio. In recent years, all of his designs have demonstrated that he is an architect with a strong sense of social responsibility.

Looking at Hou Liang's work as a whole, it becomes apparent that he is consistent in his pursuit of a kind of new architectural order called a 'nebula' (literally, an intermittently appearing cloud of interstellar dust and gas). He is fascinated by spatial architecture and inspired by the naturally changing composition of nebula clouds. His architectural designs not only present a process of materialization, but they also create a spatial experience with inner meaning.

Hou Liang has gained enormous experience from entering a high number of winning proposals in international architecture competitions. Examples of his work include the Seoul Performing Arts Centre (2005), the Tsunami Memorial, Thailand (2006) and the John Paul II Museum in Cracow, Poland (2007). Over the years he has become the most successful of the young architects participating in the international competition arena.

'Zhuan Xin Ting' is a space installation. In Chinese 'Zhuan Xin' means 'revolving mind' and the pavilion contains features for capturing time and memory. The revolving pattern maps the past, present and future, enabling visitors to look at things from various angles to find different ways in which to perceive themselves.

The installation takes its inspiration from the classical Chinese cabinet similar to a European 'Wunderkammer'. However, Hou Liang decided to join the ends of the otherwise two-dimensional cabinet to form a circle, hence its name 'revolving mind'. The structure is continuous, with no beginning or end. Hou Liang also wanted to embody the endless cycle of reincarnation, inspired by the teachings of the ancient Chinese philosopher Lao Zi. The revolving 'Wunderkammer'-inspired cabinet also sets a boundary between the exterior and interior worlds. Once visitors cross its threshold they enter the inner world. The power of the installation constantly reminds us of our virtual existence.

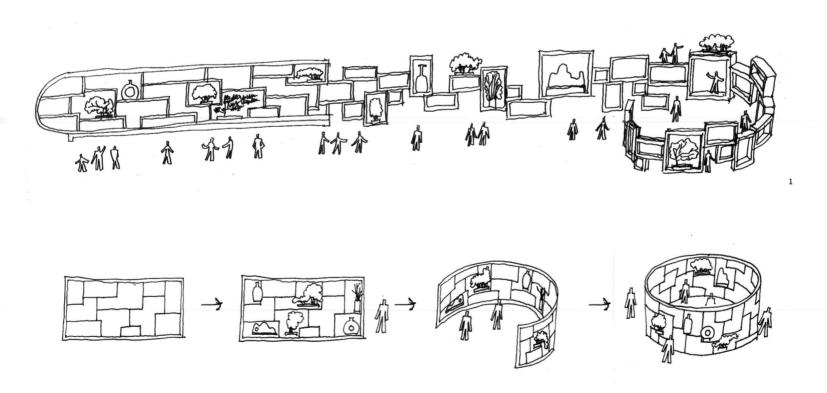

1

2

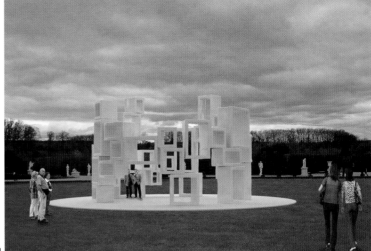

P48-P49

1. Conceptual drawing
© Hou Liang
2. Conceptual drawing
© Hou Liang
3. Model of 'Zhuan Xin Ting'
© Hou Liang
4. Digital image of 'Zhuan Xin Ting'
© Hou Liang
5. Digital image of 'Zhuan Xin Ting'
© Hou Liang

5

THE LEBANESE-OMANI CENTRE

LOCATION: **Beirut, Republic of Lebanon**
ARCHITECT: **Hou Liang**
CONSTRUCTION PERIOD: **2009**
SITE AREA: **15,294 m²**
CLIENT: **Ministry of Culture, Republic of Lebanon**

DESCRIPTION Because of its hot, dry climate, the main building type in the Middle East is closed and self-contained. In keeping with this style, the Lebanese-Omani Centre was designed as a box shape. From the exterior, it looks not unlike the local buildings, a closed box with small windows, but in fact it is an open building that is closely linked to its surroundings.

Windows are traditionally used to provide light and ventilation. In this building, the window is intended to function beyond its original use. It might be a place for temporary art shows, for a viewing deck or a planted balcony, for chatting or reading, or simply for relaxing. It is a window, but it is also a public space. Similarly, the shapes of the windows could also be flexible and variable as an aesthetic element, interacting with the façade and the surrounding space. Changing windows can be used to express the building's special function and to distinguish it from the surrounding structures. So, in this building, a window is not just a window, it is more like an apparatus, blending and mutating into different building components. Here, a window can be a programmed space or a simple lighting device, both interactive and complementary.

P50-P51
1. Digital image of the Lebanese-Omani Centre
© Hou Liang
2. Concept and elevation
© Hou Liang
3. Digital image of the Lebanese-Omani Centre by night
© Hou Liang

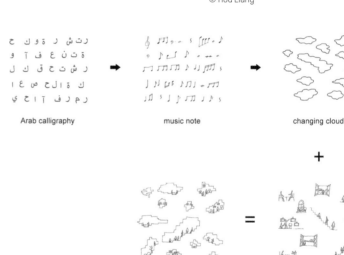

Arab calligraphy → music note → changing cloud

+

multiple purpose windows = extended programme

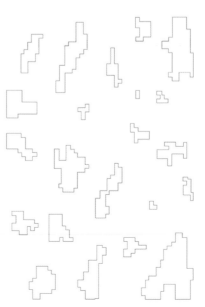

urban landscape:
vertically extended into art center

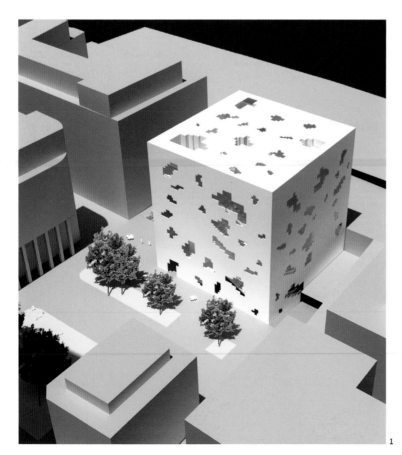

1

3

TSUNAMI MEMORIAL

LOCATION: **Phang Nga, Thailand**
ARCHITECT: **Hou Liang**
PROJECT: **2006**
BUILDING AREA: **8,000 m²**
CLIENT: **Sub-committee for the Tsunami Memorial Project**
COMPETITION: **international design competition finalist**

P52–P53
1. Digital image
© Hou Liang
2. Digital image of the interior
© Hou Liang
3. Digital image of the interior
© Hou Liang
4. Cross-section
© Hou Liang

DESCRIPTION Let us lay a wreath close to the Andaman Sea, to remember our lost sisters and brothers, mothers and fathers…
Welcome to this building open to every one, for all we believed, we pray for a better world…
Thanks to all the people who generously rescued us. Please hold my hands, to build a human fence.
After all, we all need one another.

To minimize the visual impact on the structure's natural surroundings, the site has been limited to an area 56 metres in diameter. Twelve small towers composed of stacked white prisms lean against one another, enclosing a tranquil platform made from polished stone. Inside this open-air forum, visitors can rest, worship and stage events. Within the encircling towers, people can visit the museum, attend lectures and pray according to their beliefs. Views of the memorial's guardians – Thailand's lush forest and the sea – can be seen from the tops of the towers. The memorial is intended not only to commemorate the disaster, but also to inspire hope, optimism and an appreciation of nature in current and future generations.

4

HU Yue: Restoring Outdated Buildings for the Contemporary Era

Before the alterations by the architect Hu Yue, Shanghai Qingpu Stadium and Training Hall were dilapidated and shabby. Constructed and extended in the early 1980s, the buildings are situated in the old urban area of Qingpu District, Shanghai. Similar in their design, they lacked the appeal that such buildings should possess, although it would be wrong to say that they lack any sense of history, for they were the products of their age. Before reconstruction, the interior facilities of both buildings had become almost obsolete. The client entrusted the architect to alter the external appearance of the Stadium and the Training Hall, improving their architectural image and style to bring them into line with current aesthetic standards. The interior facilities and equipment in both buildings were also to be partially altered and improved.

The reconstructed buildings have the appearance of a huge ivory-coloured, semi-glossy woven basket. Hu Yue used a very common building material – polycarbonate panels – which have a light appearance, are simple to use and relatively cheap. The weaving method used on the buildings' internal and external walls was popular in international building circles at least twenty years ago. However, the difference here is that Hu Yue has re-appropriated the techniques of handicrafts in his building method. It should be emphasized that this is not a matter of borrowing but more of conversion. In the course of this conversion the most aesthetic structures and elements have been enlarged. The weaving method, by which the vertical and horizontal polycarbonate panels have been skilfully arranged to form a reflective surface, creates a dynamic visual effect and gives the structure the appearance of a work of art. It is hard to believe that these polycarbonate panels, with double-sided UV-resistance, are only 4.5 mm thick.

In terms of the reconstruction project, three different materials are used for the cladding, including polycarbonate panels on the top layer and aluminum alloy perforated plates on the bottom layer, with local aluminum alloy square piping used throughout. Following the concept of an 'open coat', the intention was that the building's façade should reflect as much light as possible, filling the interior with natural light. In contrast to the indifferent design of the original buildings, several three-dimensional rectangles are positioned like randomly placed containers to form the entrance. This architectural design restores a thirty-year-old building, which might otherwise have been 'retired', into the first tier of new buildings.

RENOVATION OF QINGPU STADIUM AND TRAINING HALL, SHANGHAI

P54-P55
1. Panoramic view of the Training Hall
   © Fu Xing
2. South-east corner of the Training Hall
   © Fu Xing

P56-P57
1. East entrance of the Training Hall
   © Fu Xing
2. Digital image of the design
   © Hu Yue studio
3. Detail of the competition hall in the Stadium
   © Fu Xing

LOCATION: **Qingpu District, Shanghai, China**
ARCHITECTS: **Hu Yue, Tai Fangqing**
ENGINEERS: **Zhang Yanpeng, Li Hui**
ELECTRICAL AND MECHANICAL ENGINEERS: **Xue Shazhou, Wei Shen**
STRUCTURAL ENGINEER: **Huiying Liu**
CONSTRUCTION PERIOD: **2006–2008**
SITE AREA: **6,000 m²**
BUILDING AREA: **8,100 m²**
CLIENT: **The Municipal Sports Administration of Qingpu District, Shanghai**
USE: **fitness**

DESCRIPTION The Qingpu Stadium and Training Hall are located in an old urban area – Qingpu District, Shanghai – and were built and extended in the 1980s. The two buildings lacked any sense of contemporary style and shape, especially in the tapered external walls and semicircular entrance canopy of the Stadium and the tapered external walls, cambered glass curtain wall and exterior stairway of the Training Hall. The indoor facilities in the two building were out-dated. The client commissioned the architect to renovate the exterior of the Stadium and Training Hall, to bring the shape and style of the buildings to a higher standard, and partially to renew the interior facilities and equipment in the two buildings to improve their functionality.

The renovation project faced many difficulties, mainly involving lack of funding and practical problems. In view of the limited gross investment, the structure, façades, external appearance of the buildings and the indoor facilities in the Stadium were renovated rather than being rebuilt and the interior facilities in the Training Hall were only partially improved. The impact on the existing main structure of the buildings was minimal.

The exteriors of the buildings were renovated by modifying their tapered shape. The buildings were enclosed in a new envelope, enhancing the geometry of the shape and livening up the overall structure. Inside the Stadium, the facilities for small-scale sports fixtures were improved, the spectators' stands were rebuilt and auxiliary spaces and services for audiences were added.

The new envelope was constructed using three materials: polycarbonate plates for the top layer and perforated aluminium alloy plates for the bottom layer, with square aluminium alloy tubes in various places. Although polycarbonate plates are not commonly used in buildings, utilizing a single-layer plate design on building façades creates a unique effect. Polycarbonate plates are light in weight, safe, simple in structure, do not necessitate major modifications to the main structure and are relatively cheap. In addition, the transparency of polycarbonate plates can meet the requirement for interior natural lighting. The single-layer polycarbonate plates used for this project were 4.5 mm thick, in ivory-white with ultraviolet resistance on both sides and matt surfaces. The polycarbonate plates were tightly and securely connected in both horizontal and vertical directions using a weaving technique providing an 'open coat' to the building. The texture of the polycarbonate plates contributed a modern aesthetic to the building, in keeping with the urban environment.

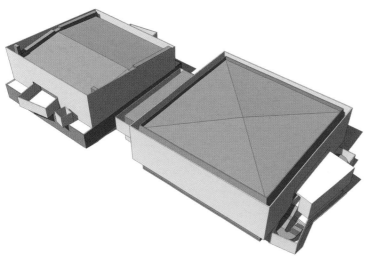

3

LI Xinggang: Research + Design

Li Xinggang has gained a high reputation in China following his contribution to the National Stadium for the Beijing Olympics, for which he was chief architectural consultant in collaboration with the international architects Herzog & de Meuron. But he prefers to talk about one of his own works, the Renovation Project No. B59 – 1 Fuxinglu, Beijing, which he designed in his own time while working on the 'Bird's Nest' (the nickname for the National Stadium). After working for several months with Herzog & de Meuron, Li set up his own studio. Inspired by this collaboration, Li tried to apply a new working method 'Research + Design' to the Fuxinglu project, in which the design is developed through research, with an emphasis on creativity based on analysis.

Renovation Project No. B59 – 1 Fuxinglu, Beijing, is a project to convert a concrete structure built in the 1990s into a small urban complex of restaurants, offices and a gallery. As the client wanted the original concrete building to remain intact, Li decided to use a metal-mesh curtain wall to complement the existing irregular column structure and its differing heights. As a means of dealing with the exterior rhombus-shaped frame and the multi-function interiors, four types of enamel glazing with different degrees of transparency were used on the

façade. The metal frame was key to the introduction of more freedom in the renovation, turning the curtain-wall system into an envelope with multiple spaces. Moreover, it became possible to incorporate a vertical garden to the west of the building. The former staircase was converted into a gallery.

A great deal of analysis work went into the design concept. Li also carried out lighting experiments and mock-ups for the curtain-wall system. It is not a big project, but Li and his studio used it as the first trial for introducing the 'Research + Design' approach into their architectural practice.

P58-P59
1. Detail of the façade of No. B59 - 1 Fuxinglu
   © Zhang Guangyuan
2. Exterior façade
   © Zhang Guangyuan

1   58

RENOVATION PROJECT NO. B59 – 1 FUXINGLU

LOCATION: **Beijing, China**
ARCHITECT: **Li Xinggang**
PROJECT TEAM: **Tan Zeyang, Zhang Yinxuan, Fu Bangbao / Atelier Li Xinggang, China Architecture Design & Research Group**
STRUCTURAL ENGINEERING: **China Building Standard Design & Research Institute (structural consultant) + Zhuhai Jingyi Glass Engineering Co. Ltd. (curtain-wall consultant)**
CONSTRUCTION PERIOD: **2004–2006**
BUILDING AREA (AFTER RENOVATION): **5,402 m²**
CLIENT: **WanYeYuan Real Estate Development Co. Ltd., Beijing**
USE: **restaurant, gallery, offices**

DESCRIPTION The renovation project, No. B59 – 1 Fuxinglu is located along the extension line of West Chang'an Avenue. It is a reconstruction of a nine-storey office building with a frame structure built in the early 1990s. The project improved the building's functionality, interior space and appearance while retaining the original structure, function and facilities.

P60-P61
1. Interior of the gallery
  © Zhang Guangyuan
2. Interior
  © Zhang Guangyuan
3. The façade by night
  © Zhang Guangyuan

P62-P63
  Main entrance
  © Zhang Guangyuan

1

2

3

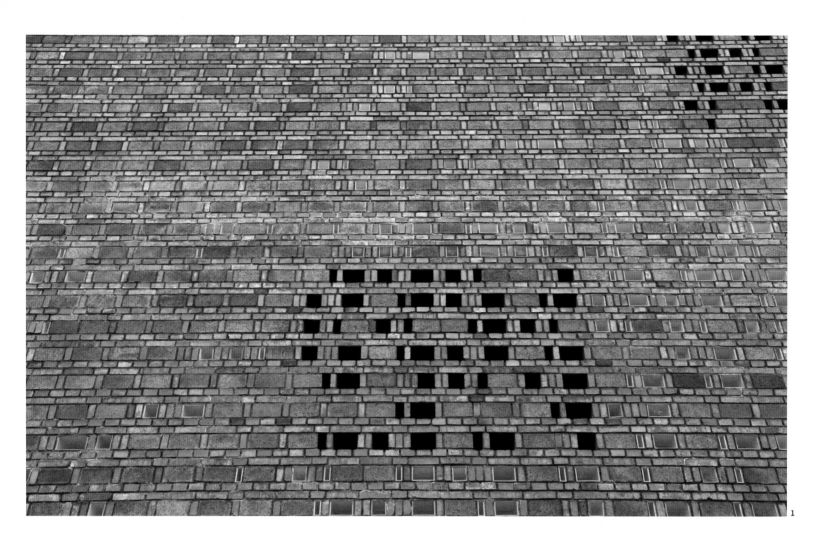

3

4

JIANCHUAN JINGJIAN AND EARTHQUAKE MUSEUM

P64-P65
1. Detail of the exterior brick wall
© Li Xinggang
2. West façade of the museum
© Li Xinggang
3. The courtyard
© Li Xinggang
4. Interior of the museum
© Li Xinggang

LOCATION: **Anren, Sichuan Province, China**
ARCHITECT: **Li Xinggang**
PROJECT TEAM: **Fu Bangbao, Zhang Yinxuan, Liu Aihua, Zhong Peng, Dong Xuan / Atelier Li Xinggang, China Architecture Design & Research Group**
STRUCTURAL ENGINEERING: **China Architecture Design & Research Group**
CONSTRUCTION PERIOD: **2004–2009**
SITE AREA: **3,847 m²**
BUILDING AREA: **6,098 m²**
CLIENT: **Sichuan Anren Jianchuan Cultural Industry Development Co. Ltd.**
USE: **exhibitions about the Cultural Revolution and relics from the Wenchuan earthquake**

DESCRIPTION Using the traditional model of mixing business with housing in the old town of Anren, this project fulfils optimal retail practice. The existing shops along the streets constitute the first layer of a three-dimensional museum complex. The vacant land at the back becomes a garden for the museum building, breaking down the boundaries between the museum and retail spaces. The main route through the museum leads visitors through a 'twin corridor' (a full corridor divided by building a wall along its central axis) and 'pavilions', allowing them both to appreciate the exhibits and to admire the garden.

Inside the museum, rotating mirror-doors are set at the junctions of the 'twin corridor'. The number of mirror-doors used increases progressively as the route proceeds through the museum, changing the rhythm of the space. The 'twin corridor' becomes a huge, complex space, like the inside of a periscope. Lured by the multiple reflections, the visitors start to feel as though they are involved in an intriguing game. In the context of this stimulating environment, visitors can explore a recent period of Chinese history – the Cultural Revolution.

The three main materials used in this structure are timber, concrete and brick. The design is enriched by the use of traditional bricklaying patterns. The brick walls support the cantilever and different patterns, with various degrees of transparency, are used according to the requirements of the different spaces, to suit the need for light, air, views or privacy.

ELEVATED METRO STATIONS

LOCATION: **Beijing, China**
ARCHITECTS: **Li Xinggang, Zhang Yinxuan, Zhang Zhe, Zhang Yuting, Zheng Shiwei, Zhao Guoqiu, Lu Yuhan, Bai Fang**
PROJECT TEAM: **China Architecture Design & Research Group**
STRUCTURAL ENGINEERING: **China Architecture Design & Research Group**
CONSTRUCTION PERIOD: **2009–2010**
SITE AREA: **1,280 m²**
BUILDING AREA: **standard station: 6,000 m² / interchange station: 12,970 m²**
CLIENT: **Beijing MTR Construction Administration Corporation**
USE: **Metro station**

DESCRIPTION There are six elevated stations along the Beijing Metro Changping Line (Phase 1). Four of them are standard stations and the other two are interchange stations. The landscape design is based on the theme of 'one line, one view'. The use of the same materials and a unified design for the façades of the stations emphasizes the attributes of simplicity, purity and fluency. In addition, the design and construction of the stations have been further integrated through the use of a modularized, standardized and pre-manufactured system.

As 'island stations', the standard elevated stations have been constructed from a seamless steel frame with a hexagonal section and with screen-printed etched glass as a façade material. The interchange stations use the same materials and designs with only slight variations, leading to the desirable scenario of 'one line, one view'. Other architectural components, such as the entrances to the platforms, stairs and awnings, are designed using the same vernacular. The excellent use of well-established construction technology gives the station façades a unique and appealing appearance.

P66–P67
1. Single-volume station
   © Li Xinggang Studio
2. Model of the interior
   © Fang Zhenning
3. Cross-section model
   © Fang Zhenning
4. Model of one end of the elevated station
   © Fang Zhenning
5. Twin-volume interchange station
   © Li Xinggang Studio

3

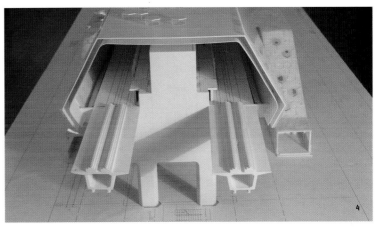

4

LIANG Jingyu: Conceptualization through Contemplation

Liang Jingyu, chief architect at Approach Architecture Studio, asserts that he is not only an architect but also a games designer. Liang formerly worked at Electronic Arts, America's largest games company, and is part of the 'returnee' generation of Chinese who have studied and lived overseas – in Liang's case, Canada – before returning to China.

Liang's contemplative working process reveals the intense scrutiny to which he subjects all of his projects. This would hardly be worth mentioning, but the majority of architects in China are unaware of how such innovative work is produced. No matter how many designs they create, familiar elements keep cropping up because many of them seek their inspiration in the work of more successful architects. Even some of China's better-known architects have yet to develop a discernible individual style – although the pressure on Chinese architects to create their own style is becoming a serious business.

Liang Jingyu's work caught our attention because it jumped out from a mediocre field. Although the source of Liang's inspiration is often unclear, the ultimate verdict must be simply that work like his has never been seen before. In today's globalized, digitized world, with its torrents of information, it is nearly impossible to create a design that has not been influenced by others – unless the conceptualization comes from a deeper level of awareness. Liang says he approaches his designs by first considering the problems to be resolved by whatever it is that he is designing. He forces himself to spend hours or days on end contemplating his unfinished designs until inspiration strikes.

Liang has participated in a number of design projects, of which his 2008 church, in the suburban Fangshan District of Beijing, is perhaps the most significant. Although Liang himself was dissatisfied with the completed church, whose owner made his own modifications to the design, the consideration and thought that Liang put into its design alone has considerable value.

The church was designed for Chinese Catholics. Liang drew from Chinese temples for his inspiration in the design of the space, the form and the lighting for the building. The changing seasons were another major element in Liang's plan for the church and its surroundings and he incorporated fallen leaves, raindrops, snowflakes and ice crystals from a nearby pond as design motifs. As in the traditional design of Chinese gardens, architecture here serves merely as a frame for nature. The most noticeable features of the church are the merging of the vertically extending tower and the horizontally extending building into the shape of a rising and falling wave. An early sketch by Liang shows the basic structure of the building, which takes its origin from a farmhouse on the outskirts of Beijing. Thus we may see from Liang's design that while the faith may come from the West, the spirit of the building comes from an appreciation of local architecture.

P68-P69
1. Early conceptual models for Suburban Church
© Liang Jingyu
2. View of the building
© Liang Jingyu

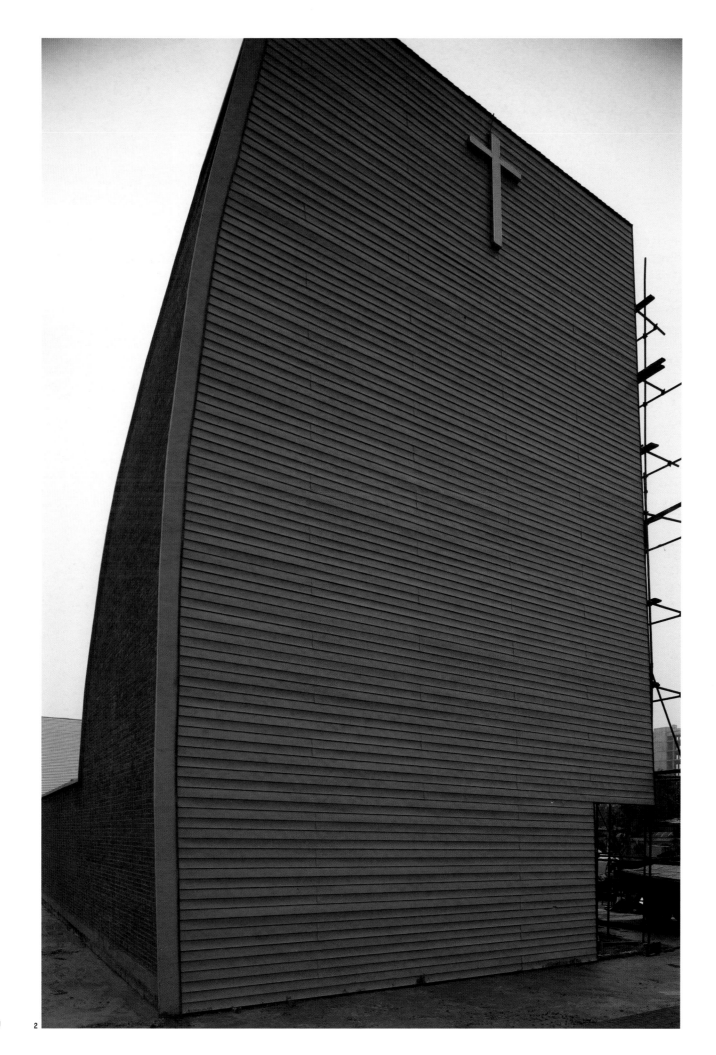

2

SUBURBAN CHURCH

LOCATION: **Fangshan District, Beijing, China**
ARCHITECT: **Liang Jingyu / Approach Architecture Studio**
PROJECT TEAM: **Gu Wei, Peng Xiaohu, Li Honglei, Zhou Yuan, Ying Gefei**
STRUCTURAL ENGINEERING: **Jiuyuan Tri-Star Architects Partnership**
CONSTRUCTION PERIOD: **2008**

DESCRIPTION This project is located in the Fangshan District of Beijing. The church is situated on a corner of the main intersection in a large residential community. Both high-rise towers and low-rise commercial outlets border the site.

The fact that the church is built for Chinese Christians presents the architect with the opportunity to question the tradition of Western church design (especially the Gothic style). To emphasize the spirit of nature, inspiration is drawn from Chinese temples in terms of space, form and light. Materials are chosen carefully for the way in which they fade or age over time. Consideration for ageing and fading are also important elements in the courtyard and landscape design. Fallen leaves, raindrops, snowflakes and ice crystals from the pond are treated as design elements. Drawing on the philosophy of the classic Chinese garden, the building itself merely acts as a frame for nature.

P70-P71
1. Early sketch
© Liang Jingyu
2. Final model
© Liang Jingyu
3. View of the building
© Liang Jingyu
4. Final model
© Liang Jingyu

1

2

IBERIA CENTRE FOR CONTEMPORARY ART

LOCATION: **798 Art District, Beijing, China**
ARCHITECT: **Liang Jingyu / Approach Architecture Studio**
ART DIRECTOR: **Lu Qiong**
PROJECT TEAM: **Peng Xiaohu, Zhao Ning, Li Honglei, Yang Jieqing, Zhou Yuan, Gu Wei**
STRUCTURAL ENGINEERING: **Jiuyuan Tri-Star Architects Partnership**
CONSTRUCTION PERIOD: **2007–2008**
BUILDING AREA: **3,000 m²**

DESCRIPTION The Iberia Centre for Contemporary Art is a re-development project located in the 798 Art District of Beijing. The original site was composed of a group of industrial buildings, of which the largest is around 1,000 m² with ceilings 8 to 11 metres high.

The concept of the re-development was to convert these discrete buildings into an integrated art exhibition space while retaining their industrial appearance. A 50-metre-long brick wall was introduced at street level to link the three buildings into a single continuous façade. The new façade does not replace the original ones, but interacts with them by means of its shape and tectonic concept.

The interior walls were preserved while several new function boxes were inserted into the lofty space. Besides the exhibition space, the building now includes offices, a library, an auditorium, a café and an art shop.

P72-P73
1. View of the entrance
   © Liang Jingyu
2. Model
   © Liang Jingyu
3. Exterior of the café
   © Liang Jingyu

P74-P75
1. The front hall of Iberia Centre
   © Fang Zhenning
2. Interior of Iberia Centre
   © Fang Zhenning
3. Interior of Iberia Centre
   © Fang Zhenning

2

3

LIU Jiakun: The 'Rebirth Brick'

The purpose of architecture is to resolve man's relationship with the natural world by creating physical spaces. The most basic function of any architecture is to shelter. Architecture not only provides protection from the elements, it also co-exists with the natural world. This is the essence of architecture.

The devastating earthquake that struck Wenchuan, China on 12 May 2008 forced architects into an extreme situation. Faced with the enormous reconstruction work needed in the aftermath of the large-scale clean up, architectural experiments and studies done during a time of stability seemed redundant. At this point in history, architects found themselves under great pressure to act swiftly and to provide help where it was most needed. Liu Jiakun was the first architect in China to respond to this change in priorities. Immediately after the earthquake he dedicated himself to a series of volunteering projects and activities. Acting on his moral principles and social conscience, he has become the most notable and highly respected architect in China.

Liu Jiakun's 'rebirth brick' was exhibited at the 2008 Venice Biennale. The idea for the 'rebirth brick' was not prompted by its capacity for use in further applications; it was the direct result of a moral conscience. The concept allows the abundance of abandoned materials to be 'reborn' under restricted economic conditions, but most importantly it allows the regeneration of public spirit and emotions in the process of reconstruction. It is only the similarities in the nature of earthquake wreckage and city construction debris that created the possibility of further architectural applications.

The key point of the 'rebirth brick plan' is to use building debris from the earthquake as the main component of a new building material. Straw is added to the rubble, which is then mixed with cement to produce a light brick. The advantage of this method is that it makes use of existing local brick production techniques and equipment, allowing bricks to be produced easily and quickly by the local people themselves. The 'rebirth brick' is not a registered product and thus it is not restricted by any legal limitations.

Because there is no specific category for this kind of brick in the National Standard, 'rebirth brick' temporarily falls under the group of 'concrete hollow blocks' for strength testing purposes. The result complies with the standard required for filled-wall construction, although its long-term structural integrity is yet to be tested through time. Currently, with quite basic equipment, the 'rebirth brick' can be produced in great quantities and to a very high standard. It can also be used to create load-bearing brick walls.

Liu Jiakun's work has been published in many books and publications about Chinese contemporary architecture, including a+u, AV, area, MADE IN CHINA and AR. He has also given lectures at MIT in Cambridge, Massachusetts and the Royal College of Art in London, as well as numerous Chinese universities.

1

2

3

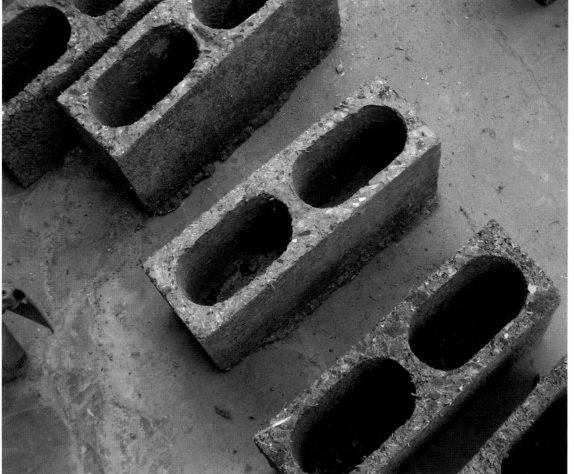

P76-P77

1. At the 11th Venice Architecture Biennale
2008
© Fang Zhenning

2. At the 11th Venice Architecture Biennale
2008
© Fang Zhenning

3. Self-build village house constructed from
solid 'rebirth brick'
© Jiakun Architects

4. Solid grey 'rebirth brick'
© Jiakun Architects

P78-P79

1. Liu Jiakun in the 512 Wenchuan earthquake
disaster zone
© Jiakun Architects

2. Manufacturing the 'rebirth brick'
© Jiakun Architects

3. Detail of the structure of 'rebirth brick'
© Jiakun Architects

LUYEYUAN STONE SCULPTURE ART MUSEUM

LOCATION: **Chengdu, Sichuan Province, China**
ARCHITECTS: **Liu Jiakun, Wang Lun**
STRUCTURAL ENGINEERING: **Zhao Ruixiang**
CONSTRUCTION PERIOD: **2001–2002**
SITE AREA: **6,670 m²**
BUILDING AREA: **1,100 m²**
CLIENT: **The Labour Union of XiangCai Securities**
USE: **private museum**

DESCRIPTION The word *Mrgadava* is derived from the Chinese characters 'Lu Ye', meaning 'field of the running deer', a significant concept in Buddhist belief. Along the road to the museum is displayed an extensive collection of Buddhist stone carvings from the Han Dynasty (206 BC–AD 220) to the Song Dynasty (AD 960–1125). On a site of 900 m² the museum is constructed in concrete and arranged over two floors. The upper gallery incorporates a roof garden. An external stairway provides access to a viewing platform from which the river and surrounding landscape can be admired. On the ground floor, the architect has created a small multi-functional space, an office and more galleries. Liu Jiakun has used the same rough concrete walls for both internal and external walls of the museum. In order to protect the works of art from the sun, the windows are unusually long in shape.

The Chinese architect has used local materials to create a poetic space and a surrounding landscape that helps visitors to understand the spiritual value of ancient art. This private museum of carved stone artefacts is one of the most representative buildings of its kind in China.

1

P80–P81
1. Entrance ramp
© Jiakun Architects
2. Interior view
© Jiakun Architects
3. Exit
© Jiakun Architects
4. Rooftop landscape with pool
© Fang Zhenning

P82–P83
1. Path through the surrounding landscape
© Jiakun Architects
2. Garden with cascading water
© Fang Zhenning
3. Exterior view
© Jiakun Architects
4. Entrance ramp
© Fang Zhenning

2

3

1

2

HU HUISHAN MEMORIAL HOUSE

P84-P85
1. Liu Jiakun meeting Hu Huishan's family
   © Jiakun Architects
2. Entrance
   © Jiakun Architects
3. Commemorative exhibits
   © Jiakun Architects

LOCATION: **Dayi, Anren County, Sichuan Province, China**
ARCHITECTS: **Liu Jiakun, Luo Ming, Sun En, Zhang Tong**
STRUCTURAL ENGINEERING: **Liu Su**
CONSTRUCTION PERIOD: **2009**
SITE AREA: **58 m²**
BUILDING AREA: **19 m²**
CLIENT: **sponsored by Jiakun Architects Studio**
USE: **memorial**

DESCRIPTION The Hu Huishan Memorial House is located in a small glade next to the '512 Earthquake Memorial Hall' at the Jianchuan Museum Complex in Anren. It is small and normal, just like the girl for whom it was built. Hu Huishan was an ordinary secondary school student during her lifetime. In the 512 earthquake disaster, she was buried in the collapsed building. The design of Hu Huishan Memorial takes as its prototype the pitched roofs of makeshift tents. The exterior base and interior are paved with red brick and the surfaces are plastered in the style of local village houses. The interior is painted in Hu Huishan's favourite colour, pink. A few commemorative exhibits are displayed on the walls, which sparely document the girl's short life. This memorial is built for Hu Huishan, but it also commemorates ordinary lives in general – for it is only by treasuring the ordinary that the foundation can be laid for the nation's revival.

1

2

LÜ Pinjing:
The Cosmopolitan Campus

The design of school buildings has not occupied a prominent position in recent Chinese architectural history, since schools were essentially planned and built according to the same template. This began to change at the end of the last century, in the Pudong District of Shanghai, when the New York-based firm of Pei Cobb Freed & Partners, former home to I.M. Pei, designed the garden-like China Europe International Business School, whose campus was a fresh reinterpretation of school design in Chinese architecture.

In 2007 came another innovative campus, designed by a team led by architect and educator Lü Pinjing for the Shandong University of Art and Design, in the Changqing District of Jinan, Shandong Province. Unlike the Pei Cobb Freed design, this campus was conceived with urban life in mind.

The campus is like a miniature city, recalling the Ideal City of Chaux designed by the French architect Claude-Nicolas Ledoux (1736–1806) in 1773–79 (published in 1804), incorporating Ledoux's *Saline Royale Arc et Senans*. Ledoux's design had a circular government building as its centre, with all the other buildings radiating out from it in a semicircle. Lü's own design is also arranged in a great semicircle. To the east are the school's gallery, museum, administrative building, library and conference hall. To the west are trapezoidal classrooms, classroom blocks and general studios. The most direct impression after seeing Lü's design is that it more closely resembles an industrial building complex than a campus.

Industrial architecture rejects all ornamental elements; it is purely functional and seeks, like a machine, efficiently to deploy different components in a restricted space. Rationality is the factor most prized in industrial architecture, for it ensures maximum productivity from the industry it houses. Campuses, similarly, are a venue for training individuals, in a limited amount of time, to a set curriculum designed to produce professionals. Like industrial complexes, campuses also require strict organization and arrangement. The elevation of rationality in modern campus architecture can therefore be said to bear a certain degree of similarity to industrial architecture in its composition.

Lü Pinjing believes that a relatively dense arrangement of buildings and multifunctional design is crucial in creating a city-like environment in which teachers and students can live and work. Rather than opting for the inflexible, scattered classroom arrangements that are common in school campuses, or falling into the habit of arranging teaching blocks around a central field, Lü chose to connect the multifunctional spaces organically, to express the personality of the arts school and to integrate normally disparate functions. By these means, he forms

an architectural unit as though he were casting and then compressing a gigantic ingot, providing a visual stimulus to the creativity of the teachers and students who live and work here.

Lü's 'campus city' is home to indoor 'streets' connecting galleries, reading rooms, offices, classrooms and stores. Internal 'streets and plazas' cut across the boundaries between different departments and workshops, just as one would find in a city. In his vision, the campus space no longer emphasizes the superior/subordinate relationship between teacher and student, but rather places all of its 'citizens' on an equal footing, the intersecting streets and alleys giving rise to a familiar, neighbourly atmosphere.

P86-P87
1. Terraces around the school playing-fields
at Shandong University
© Fang Zhenning
2. The lift-tower
© Fang Zhenning

NEW CAMPUS FOR SHANDONG UNIVERSITY OF ART AND DESIGN

LOCATION: **Changqing District, Jinan, China**
ARCHITECT: **Lü Pinjing**
PROJECT TEAM: **Beijing Yongmao Architects' Office, Han Wenqiang, Chen Yu, Xue Yanbo, Huang Hui, Zhou Yufang**
STRUCTURAL ENGINEERING: **Shandong Architectural Design Institute**
CONSTRUCTION PERIOD: **2004–2007**
SITE AREA: **about 555,333.6 m²**
BUILDING AREA: **250,000 m²**
CLIENT: **Shandong University of Art and Design**
USE: **education**

DESCRIPTION The new campus of the Shandong University of Art and Design combines a dense architectural layout with comprehensive multi-functionality. It is like a mini-city for the students and faculty members who live there. On the campus, various functional spaces (including an exhibition hall, reading rooms, an office building, lecture theatres and shops) are connected and divided by indoor 'streets' and by 'squares'. There is also a cluster of workshops for training purposes that function like the high street of a city.

P88-P89
1. Tower with glass staircase
© Fang Zhenning
2. Workshop for students to practise what they learn
© Fang Zhenning
3. Main teaching block
© Fang Zhenning
4. Lecture theatre
© Fang Zhenning

DESIGN BUILDING, CENTRAL ACADEMY OF FINE ARTS

P90-P91
1. Model
   © Fang Zhenning
2. Model
   © Fang Zhenning
3. Model
   © Fang Zhenning

LOCATION: **Chaoyang District, Beijing, China**
ARCHITECT: **Lü Pinjing**
CONSTRUCTION PERIOD: **2001–2002**
SITE AREA: **2,500 m²**
BUILDING AREA: **23,000 m²**
CLIENT: **Central Academy of Fine Arts, China**
USE: **education**

DESCRIPTION The spirit of traditional Chinese architecture focuses on the integration, combination and transition between inner and outer spaces. These are the design concepts on which the Design Building of the Central Academy of Fine Arts is founded. Three-storey teaching units connect with each other, creating both architectural volumes and connecting spaces, giving a sense of both substance and insubstantiality. Lecture theatres and atriums, indoor and outdoor spaces, upper and lower levels, above ground and underground – all are organically combined. The diversified use of space fulfils all the necessary requirements for the teaching of architecture, art and design students. The transit points between forms and structures provide a vast platform for numerous teaching and learning activities.

NINGDONG OFFICE BUILDING

LOCATION: **Yinchuan, Ningxia Province, China**
ARCHITECT: **Lü Pinjing**
CONSTRUCTION PERIOD: **2008–2009**
SITE AREA: **10,000 m²**
BUILDING AREA: **13,700 m²**
CLIENT: **Ningxia Coal Group Company**
USE: **offices**

DESCRIPTION Yinchuan, the capital city of Ningxia Province, is well known for its Imperial Tombs from the Xixia Kingdom. Those tombs, which are sometimes regarded as the 'pyramids of the Oriental world', reveal the glories of past history. Now there will be another striking 'pyramid' next to the imperial tombs. This new pyramid will be the control centre of China's largest coal and chemical industrial company and will undoubtedly form another milestone in Chinese contemporary architecture. By cutting and stretching different forms of architecture – using a steel supporting system with a hollow double-skinned curtain-wall system – and with the inclusion of a circular pond containing recycled water, we can surely expect an exciting and intimate but effective industrial working space in the middle of the desolate desert.

P92-P93
1. Model
© Fang Zhenning
2. Model
© Fang Zhenning
3. Model
© Fang Zhenning
4. Model
© Fang Zhenning

3

4

MA Yansong:
MAD in China

MAD is a Beijing-based design collaboration dedicated to innovation in architectural practice, landscape design and urban planning. Founded by Ma Yansong with two partners, Yosuke Hayano and Qun Dang, MAD became a leading voice in the new generation of design after Ma moved his office back to Beijing from New York in 2003. Controversy about Ma Yansong began far earlier than the founding of MAD. However, it is an undisputable fact that Ma is one of the best-known Chinese architects around the world. People often ask: 'what do you think of Ma Yansong and his design?' The wise answer would be: 'tell me who else in China deserves to be more talked about than him.' In the past two years, people have started to re-evaluate Ma Yansong and his young office, as a series of landmark buildings were constructed which demonstrated strong ideas and solid progress.

I interviewed Ma in 2001 when he was still a student in the Architecture School at Yale. Soon after that, on 11 September 2001, the attacks on the New York World Trade Centre occurred. It was an event that almost changed Ma's point of view about the world. His work 'Floating Island – Rebuilt WTC' revealed Ma's tremendous courage and talents. It was taken up by the media in China and provoked huge debate among the architects and the public.

In the first two years after Ma moved back to Beijing, he participated in almost 100 competitions, won a few of them, but did not get to make any buildings. In 2005, MAD won the first prize in a competition for a 50-storey apartment building in Mississauga Toronto for their pro- posal – the Absolute Tower – a twisting tower with 360-degree views of the urban environment. It was nicknamed Marilyn Monroe Tower by the locals and became the absolute turning point for this office, which at that time was hidden in an apartment somewhere in the city. Ma Yansong won a series of landmark commissions from government agencies and big state owned enterprises. The hierarchy in urban planning decisions was broken down as Ma turned from being a silent observer at the sidelines to being a strong voice giving opinions solicited by the city authorities. All of a sudden, architects were empowered, and Ma fully realized that power meant responsibility.

Ma Yansong and the MAD office have become the symbol of the upcom- ing architects born in the 1970s. They are challenging the architectural hierarchy with their unique concept of futurism in China and exploring a renewed understanding of nature and advanced technology. Their new project 'Urban Forest' in Chongqing, is the pioneer of the green skyscraper, a man-made symbiosis that reacts to the high density of urban life, in harmony with nature. Approaching their work from the theoretical and practical level, Ma Yansong and his design team stimulate discussion on how to change the city of today and tomorrow.

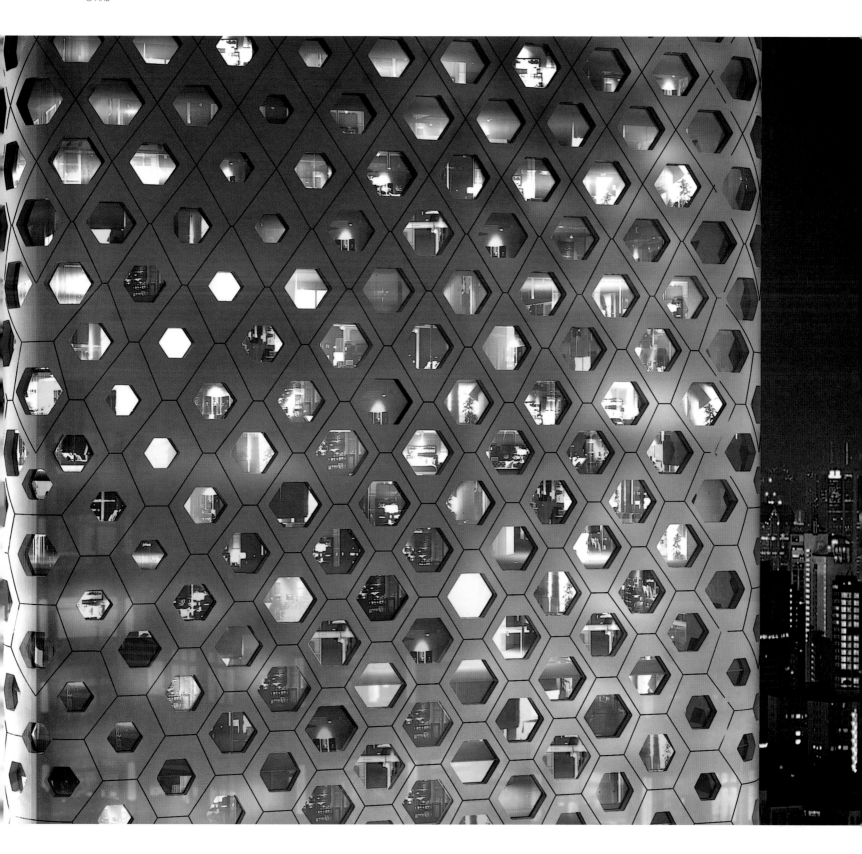

MEADOW CLUBHOUSE

LOCATION: **Ulanbutong, Inner Mongolia, China**
ARCHITECTS: **Ma Yansong / MAD, Yosuke Hayano, Qun Dang**
DESIGN TEAM: **Guntis Zingis, Zhao Wei, Yu Kui, Evone Tam, Li Peng, Louise Fiil, Wang Xingfang, Fu Changrui, Liu Xiaopu**
ASSOCIATE ENGINEERS: **Beijing YunXiang Architectural Engineering Design Company Ltd.**
CONSTRUCTION PERIOD: **2006–2008**
SITE AREA: **58,600 m²**
BUILDING AREA: **586 m²**
USE: **villa**

DESCRIPTION This project is located in a vast and beautiful landscape in the Ulanbutong region of Inner Mongolia. It comprises a group of eight weekend and holiday homes to accommodate visitors from the city seeking a rural retreat. Covered in green grass in the summer and white snow in the winter, the environment presented an unusual challenge. The buildings needed to fit seamlessly into two entirely different landscapes.

The aim of the design is to respect and respond to the landscape. A masterplan was created that identified eight totally different topographies, including such features as a cave, a tree, a hilltop or the bottom of a valley. Eight unique houses were designed to fit these topographies, with the details of each site helping to determine the

shape and form of the structure. Rather than imposing a single design across the site, such an approach allows nature to guide what is built and extends the feeling of an organic, natural retreat.

This is the first of the houses to be completed. Its external form was determined by the proximity of an existing silver birch tree, which the house encircles and whose colour the house takes as its own. The hillside location affords magnificent views across the valley and the large, sloping windows in the front façade follow the gradient of the hill. The interior is arranged over three levels descending the hill, each with a separate function (services, relaxation and sleeping) and all are connected by an intricate stairway.

3

4

P96–P97

1. Meadow Clubhouse in winter
      Photo: Daniele Dainelli © MAD
2. Meadow Clubhouse in early spring
      Photo: Vanessa Chen © MAD
3. Meadow Clubhouse in winter
      Photo: Daniele Dainelli © MAD
4. Floor plans
      © MAD

Ground floor 1:300

Ground floor 1:300

Ground floor 1:300

Upper floor 1:300

Upper floor 1:300

Upper floor 1:300

SINOSTEEL INTERNATIONAL PLAZA

LOCATION: **Tianjin, China**
ARCHITECT: **Ma Yansong / MAD**
CONSTRUCTION PERIOD: **2007–**
SCALE: **358,886 m²**
USE: **office, hotel, serviced apartments**

P98-P99
1. Study for a window
   © MAD
2. Computer image of the interior
   © MAD
3. Bird's-eye view
   © MAD

DESCRIPTION Sinosteel International Plaza is a new organic landmark for the redeveloped city of Tianjin. The design concept combines shape, structure and cultural symbolism in one repeated motif, the hexagon, which multiplies and grows across the building's façade.

This façade is made up of five different sizes of hexagonal windows, a traditional element in Chinese architecture. These windows flow across the building in an irregular, naturally occurring pattern, like multiplying cells. This device animates the façade, creating an ever-changing image of the building from every perspective. The façade also forms the structure of the building, like an exoskeleton, a sheer solid surface. This removes the need for any internal columns beyond the building's core, freeing up space within the structure for much more flexible use. This bold new solution challenges conventional construction technology, in order to achieve something unique. The varied honeycomb also improves the building's energy efficiency. Although the façade pattern at first appears random, it responds to the climatic conditions of the plot. By mapping the different airflows and the direction of the sun across the site and positioning the windows accordingly, it is possible to minimize heat loss in the winter and heat gain in the summer.

From this very simple concept, deeply rooted in ancient Chinese structures, a subtle and sensitive building will rise. Sinosteel International Plaza will create an entirely different urban landscape, softening the hard environment of the concrete city.

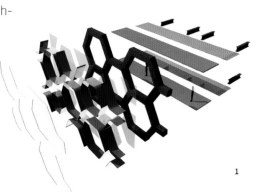

1

2

3

BEAUTIFUL MINDS 2008

LOCATION: **Ansan, Korea**
ARCHITECT: **Ma Yansong / MAD**
PROJECT TEAM: **Jtravis Bennett Russett**
DIMENSIONS: **2,340 (L) x 2,470 (W) x 2,780 (H) mm**
MATERIALS: **fibreglass, plastic, LED lighting**
USE: **urban proposal / furniture**

DESCRIPTION This project aims to promote urban intelligence. It exists at two different scales: urban scale and furniture scale, public and private, conceptual and real. Inspired by the beautiful natural landscape of Ansan, the project seeks to create something artificial and intelligent in response.

At the urban scale, this project proposes a cultural centre for Ansan. This building will represent the brain and imagination of the city, a place to celebrate and develop ideas across every intellectual discipline, from religion to artistic and scientific thought.

The building is organized as a cultural pyramid in a natural shape. Larger facilities, such as lecture halls, chapels and galleries, occupy the base of the building, grouped to mirror the patterns of the human brain: rational, mathematical facilities are located in one section of the structure, whilst intuitive, imaginative disciplines occupy the other. Smaller, more intimate learning environments are scattered above and between them, creating many opportunities for unexpected encounters and the synthesis of new ideas across intellectual boundaries.

At the very top of the tentacles can be found 'Inspiration Pods'. Suspended high above the noise, pollution and commercialism of the city, these are the 'minds' of the building. Offering a clear, objective view of the city and its culture below, the pods provide the perfect environment for students and visitors to think.

This project also exists in the material world as furniture. Here, the relationship with the object is a much more personal affair. At this scale, the structure becomes a sofa, inviting people to sit, read and learn on their own. The tentacles become lighting, providing illumination for the reader below.

At all scales, this object aims to encourage the imagination. Both building and furniture provide the same environment: a place for people to think, an environment in which to develop 'Beautiful Minds'.

3

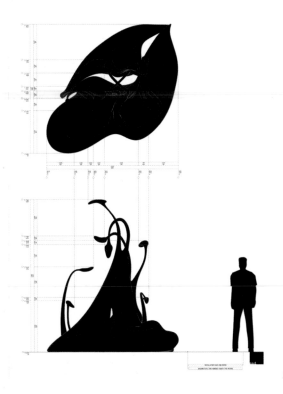

1

2

P100–P101
1. Plan and elevation
   © MAD
2. As furniture, the structure becomes a sofa
   Photo: Iwan Bann © MAD
3. This project exists at two different scales:
   urban scale and furniture scale, public and
   private, conceptual and real
   © MAD

P102–P103
At the urban scale, the project becomes a
cultural centre for Ansan
© MAD

FAKE HILLS

LOCATION: **Beihai, China**
ARCHITECT: **Ma Yansong / MAD**
PROJECT TEAM: **MAD**
CONSTRUCTION PERIOD: **2008–**
SITE AREA: **430,000 m²**
USE: **housing, offices, hotel**

DESCRIPTION Throughout China's ultra-rapid urbanization, attention has been focused on set-piece architecture such as opera houses, museums and stadiums. However these would-be icons are the exception rather than the rule. The vast majority of development in China's new cities takes the form of residential schemes, often standardized and cheap, to guarantee a quick return for the developer. Is it possible to build high-density, economically viable housing that is also architecturally innovative?

This development is located in the coastal city of Beihai, on a long, narrow waterfront site. The design concept combines the two typologies that usually define residential developments (high-rise towers or low-rise blocks) to create a bold new structure in the form of a long slab. This shape maximizes views for residents, but imposes a monolithic barrier between the waterfront and the land behind it. The solution is twofold: to cut into the slab, creating a sculpted form which mirrors the shape of the hills dominating the region's landscape, and to create openings in the structure allowing it to be penetrated by space, views and light. A further reference point is traditional Chinese architecture's obsession with nature. Rather than siting the building in a man-made garden, the structure becomes the man-made natural shape itself: fake hills for the residents to live in. The design provides both a high-density solution and a new landmark for the city.

CHONGQING URBAN FOREST

LOCATION: **Chongqing, China**
ARCHITECT: **Ma Yansong**
PROJECT TEAM: **Yu Kui, Fu Changrui, Diego Perez, Dai Pu**
CONSTRUCTION PERIOD: **2009**
SITE AREA: **7,700 m²**
BUILDING AREA: **216,000 m²**
CLIENT: **Chongqing Xinhua Bookstore Group**
USE: **retail, five-star hotel, offices**

DESCRIPTION 'Urban Forest' is not a banal working machine, but rather a man-made symbiosis that responds to high-density urban life in harmony with nature. The Urban Forest will not be determined by the redundant logic of industrial high density, but instead follows the fragile rules of nature to create a complex taxonomy of urban activities, revealing the image of the architecture of the future.

In today's high-density urban environment, the limits of urbanization are controlled and set by nature. Generic verticality is replaced by a complex range of urban activities, defined by a multiplicity of connections, detours and shortcuts. Urban activities are mixed with verdant gardens and open spaces, forming multi-layer platforms where people can reconnect with the sun, wind and natural light. All of these free-form urban-nature layers are stacked one on top of another, creating the random geometric shape of the green urban jungle, in which an organic spatial relationship is transformed into an ever-changing urban environment.

'Urban Forest' is the pioneer of the green skyscraper, a free-breathing man-made high-rise organic jungle within the urban concrete jungle.

P106-P107
1. Urban Forest is the pioneer of the green
   skyscraper
   © MAD
2. The building responds to high-density urban
   life in harmony with nature
   © MAD

P108-P109
1. Urban activities are combined with gardens
   and open spaces
   © MAD
2. Cross-sections
   © MAD

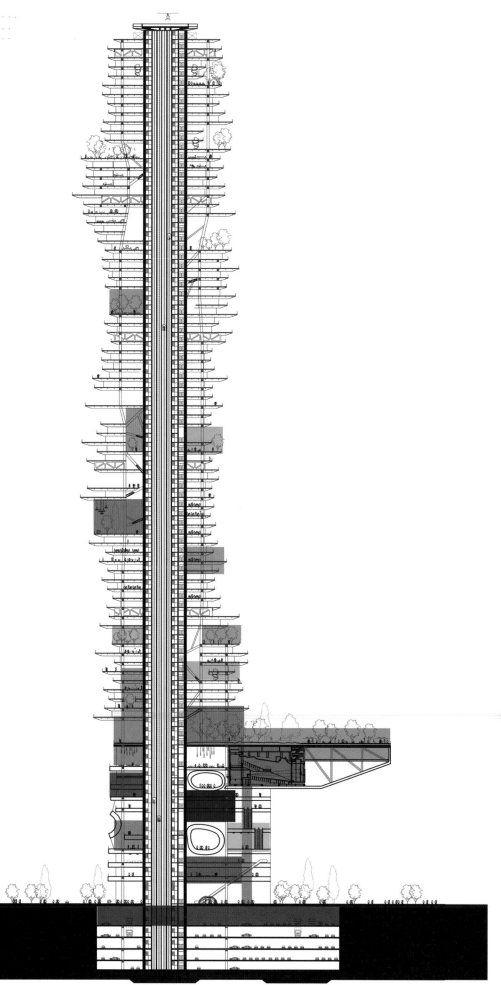

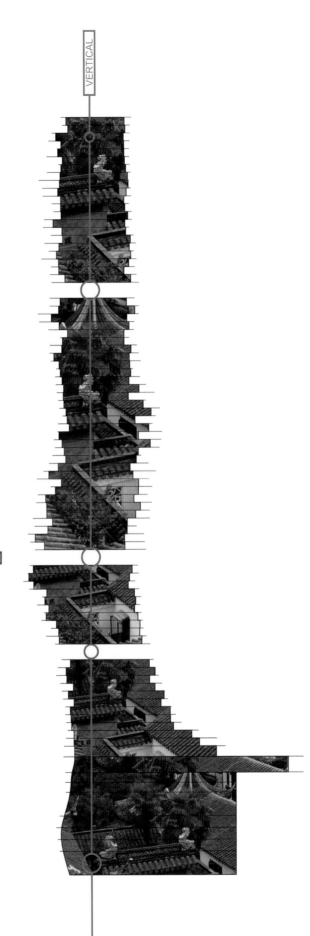

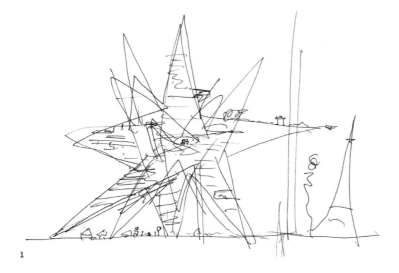

1

2

SUPERSTAR: A MOBILE CHINATOWN

Arsenale Gallery, 11th Venice Architecture Biennale
ARCHITECT: **Ma Yansong / MAD**
CONSTRUCTION PERIOD: **2008**
DIMENSIONS: **5,200 (L) x 4,800 (W) x 5,000 (H) mm**
MATERIALS: **acrylic, stainless steel**
VIDEO: **3'28"**
USE: **installation, video, computer-generated images**

DESCRIPTION A new project by MAD, 'Superstar: A Mobile Chinatown', was featured in the exhibition Uneternal City at the 11th Venice Architecture Biennale, curated by Aaron Betsky. The exhibition invited twelve young global architects to suggest interventions for an anonymous suburb of Rome, which would exploit and represent new spaces and the urban fabric of a Rome of the future. It was shown in the Arsenale, from 14 September to 23 November 2008.

MAD's proposal, the 'Superstar', takes the form of a new Chinatown. Along with shopping malls, petrol stations and branches of McDonalds, the traditional Chinatown renders all of our cities boring and alike. Composed of nothing more than streets of restaurants and fake traditional buildings it represents a kitsch image of contemporary China, devoid of real life; a historical theme park that poisons the urban space. A form of shock therapy is needed to remedy the situation.

'Superstar: A Mobile Chinatown' is MAD's response to the redundant and increasingly outdated nature of the contemporary Chinatown. Rather than being a sloppy patchwork of poor construction and nostalgia, the 'Superstar' is a fully integrated, coherent and, above all, modern upgrade of the twentieth-century Chinatown model. It is a place to enjoy oneself, to consume Chinese food, to buy quality goods and to experience cultural events; it is a place to create and to produce, where citizens can use workshops to study, design and realize their ideas.

Equally important is how this neo-community functions. 'Superstar: A Mobile Chinatown' is a benevolent virus that releases unknown energy between unprincipled changes and principled steadiness. It can land in every corner of the world, creating an exchange between a new Chinese energy and the environment in which it rests. It is self-sustaining: it grows its own food, requires no resources from the host city and recycles all of its waste; it is a living place, with authentic Chinese nature, health resorts, sports facilities and reservoirs; and it is a travelling Olympic party, that can journey to the host city every four years. There is even a digital cemetery to remember the dead. The 'Superstar' is a dream that is home to 15,000 people: there is no hierarchy, no hyponymy, but a fusion of technology and nature, the future and humanity.

P110-P111
1. Sketch by Ma Yansong
© MAD
2. 'Superstar' in New York
© MAD
3. There is no hierarchy in the 'Superstar', but a fusion of technology and nature, the future and humanity
© MAD

P112-P113
1. Five-metre-high model
© Fang Zhenning
2. 'Superstar' will provide an unexpected, ever-changing future embedded in the eternal past
© MAD
3. 'Superstar's first destination will be the suburbs of Rome
© MAD
4. 'Superstar' landing in Dubai
© MAD

1

2

3

4

HUTONG BUBBLE 32

LOCATION: **Beijing, China**
ARCHITECT: **Ma Yansong / MAD**
PROJECT TEAM: **Dai Pu**
CONSTRUCTION PERIOD: **2008**
BUILDING AREA: **130 m²**
OWNER: **private**
USE: **furniture shop**

DESCRIPTION The *hutongs* are historic poor neighbourhoods of central Beijing. Though the *hutongs* delight tourists, life for the residents is hard: they have limited private space and no indoor shower or toilet. At the same time as these residents are being re-housed by the government on the outskirts of the city, their historic homes are being occupied by the rich and by property developers who tear down the old buildings and recreate them in ersatz form.

Rather than allow the *hutongs* to become historical theme parks, we propose a more forward-looking solution. We will make super modern modifications to the fabric of the *hutongs*, either to provide new private facilities (showers, toilets, playrooms) for the current residents or to create new spaces for the wealthy to live next door. Our proposal will mix current and future lifestyles in the historic fabric.

In 2050, the lives of the people who live in the *hutongs* will be valued, rather than just the buildings themselves.

1

URBANUS: Buildings for Low-income Communities

Founded by Liu Xiaodu, Meng Yan and Wang Hui in 1999, Urbanus has opened two offices in Shenzhen and Beijing. It has been involved in nearly 300 important architecture and planning projects. Numerous completed works include those for culture, education, offices, commercial, residential, interior design, public art, landscape design, urban design and research and urban renovation and regeneration projects. Among these, 'Urban Tulou' – an affordable housing project, which was completed in 2008 – has attracted tremendous attention among architectural professionals, the media and the Chinese public.

The Chinese government recently launched a new policy for tackling the shortage of housing for families on low incomes. The plan is to build government-subsidized communities benefiting 40,070,000 people. By 2009, the government had already built new housing for about 2,500,000 families and has further building projects planned for another 7,470,000 families over the next three years. The developer of the 'Urban Tulou' project, Vanke Co., Ltd. – one of the best-known property developers in China – is leading efforts in response to government policy.

The *tulou* is a unique building type, which has its origins in the traditional dwellings from Fujian Province, China. Urbanus has creatively used this model to transform urban wastelands resulting from the rapid development of cities, building the 'Urban Tulou' within the modern city. This is a pioneering experiment in solving the problem of integrating new residents into an increasingly urbanized China.

Regarded as a building, as well as a community, the 'Urban Tulou' by Urbanus has not only inherited the culture and community spirit of the original *tulou* by creating more social opportunities for its neighbourhood, which have been in short supply in the metropolitan area, it has also been adapted to the needs of modern families by the inclusion of kitchens and bathrooms in each unit.

P118-P119
1. Green courtyard in the 'Urban Tulou'
   © Urbanus
2. Elevation
   © Urbanus

1

URBAN TULOU

LOCATION: **Guangzhou, China**
PROJECT TEAM: **Liu Xiaodu, Meng Yan, Li Da, Yin Yujun, Huang Zhiyi, Li Hui, Cheng Yun, Huang Xi, Zuo Lei**
PROJECT: **2005–2008**
CONSTRUCTION PERIOD: **2006–2008**
SITE AREA: **13,711 m²**
CLIENT: **Shenzhen Vanke Real Estate Co. Ltd.**

DESCRIPTION The *tulou* is a dwelling type that is unique to the Hakka people. It is a communal residence, combining aspects of the city and the countryside, in which living, storage, shopping, spiritual needs and public entertainment are integrated into a single structure. Traditional units in *tulou* are evenly laid out along its perimeter, like modern slab-style dormitory buildings, but with greater opportunities for social interaction. Simply copying the form and style of the *tulou* would not be a good solution; however, by learning from the *tulou*, one can help preserve community spirit among low-income families.

By introducing the 'Urban Tulou' to modern cities and by careful experimentation with both form and economy, one can transcend conventional urban design. Our experiments explored ways to incorporate the *tulou* into the existing urban fabric of the city – its green spaces, overpasses, motorways and wasteland. The cost of residual sites is quite low due to government subsidies – an important factor in developing low-income housing. The close proximity of each *tulou* building helps insulate the inhabitants from the chaos and noise outside, while creating an intimate and comfortable environment inside.

Integrating the living culture of traditional Hakka *tulou* buildings with low-income housing is not only an academic concern – there is also an important social issue too. The living conditions of those on low incomes are now gaining more public attention.

How can one effectively adapt the *tulou* for the modern city? Our research was characterized by comprehensive analyses, from the theoretical to practical application. The study examined the size, layout and functions of *tulou* buildings. We also tried to inject new urban elements into the traditional style and balance the tension between these two paradigms. In the end, we not only realized the feasibility and usefulness of the *tulou*, but we also gained experience and a deep understanding of a truly urban building type.

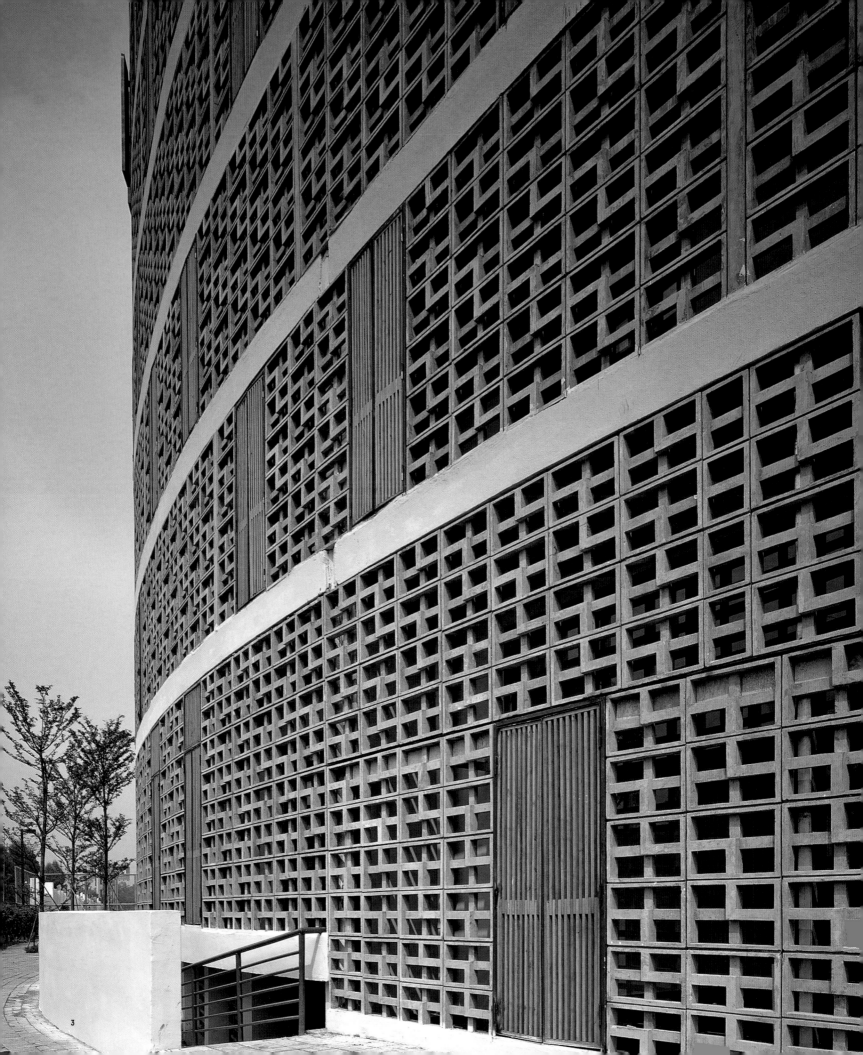

4

5

6

DAFEN ART MUSEUM

LOCATION: **Shenzhen, China**
CHIEF ARCHITECTS: **Meng Yan, Liu Xiaodu**
PROJECT TEAM: **Chen Yaoguang, Fu Zhuoheng, Zhang Yu, Ji Yuyu**
PROJECT: **2005–2006**
CONSTRUCTION PERIOD: **2007**
SITE AREA: **17,000 m²**

DESCRIPTION Dafen Village is situated in Buji Township, Longgang District, Shenzhen. Best known for its replica oil-painting workshops and manufacturers, its exports to Asia, Europe and America bring in billions of RMB (the Chinese currency) to the area each year.

The concept focuses on reinterpreting the urban and cultural associations of Dafen Village, which has long been considered a bizarre mix of pop art, bad taste and commercialism. A standard art museum would be considered out of place in the context of Dafen's peculiar urban culture. The question is whether or not it can become a breeding ground for contemporary art and take on the more challenging role of blending in with the surrounding urban fabric, in terms of spatial connections, art activities and everyday life. Therefore the strategy is to create a mix of different programmes under one roof, including art museums, galleries and shops, commercial spaces, workshops and studios. The different routes through the building's public spaces encourage interaction between its diverse functions. This sandwiching of the museum between commercial and public programmes allows for visual and spatial connections between its various activities. Exhibitions, trade, painting and living spaces occur simultaneously and can be woven into a whole new urban mechanism.

P124-P125
1. View from the upper gallery
   © Fang Zhenning
2. Skylight
   © Fang Zhenning
3. Exterior wall of artist's studio
   © Fang Zhenning
4. Rooftop artist's studio
   © Urbanus
5. Bridge linking housing to museum
   © Urbanus

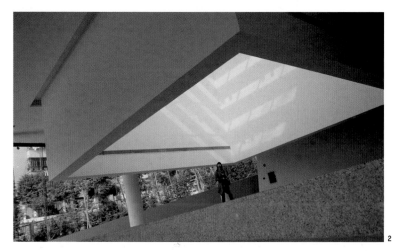

1

2

3

4

5

1

2

OCT ART AND DESIGN GALLERY

LOCATION: **Shenzhen, China**
PROJECT TEAM: **Meng Yan, Liu Xiaodu, Deng Dan, Yao Xiaowei, Cedric Yu, Cheng Yun, Guo Donghai, Wang Yanfeng**
PROJECT: **2006–2008**
CONSTRUCTION PERIOD: **2008**
SITE AREA: **2,620 m²**
CLIENT: **Shenzhen OCT Real Estate Co. Ltd.**

DESCRIPTION The site has had a rather unremarkable history. Originally constructed as a laundry warehouse for Shenzhen Bay Hotel in the early 1980s, it is situated along the main road, between a Spanish-style hotel and the He Xiangning Gallery. The warehouse itself remained unaltered for many years while the city around it was transformed. Given the significance of its location, the owner decided to remodel the warehouse in a meaningful way. For Urbanus, the remodelling of the site posed difficult questions concerning how to address the existing urban condition, and how new interventions would relate to it.
The main architectural gesture is to wrap the entire warehouse in a glass curtain wall. The pattern is created from four different sizes of hexagons. As a result, the new wall becomes a lively theatrical screen.

The geometric pattern is not merely on the surface but forms a three-dimensional matrix of intersecting elements that project into the gallery spaces, structuring the building's interior design. The result is the creation of delightful and unexpected spatial experiences.

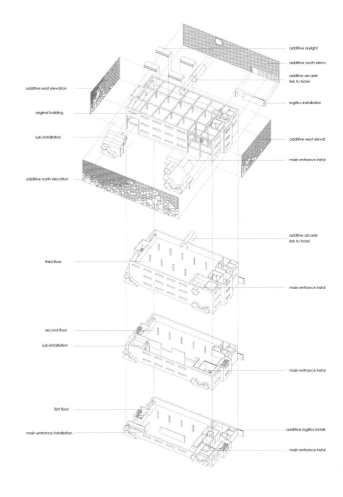

3

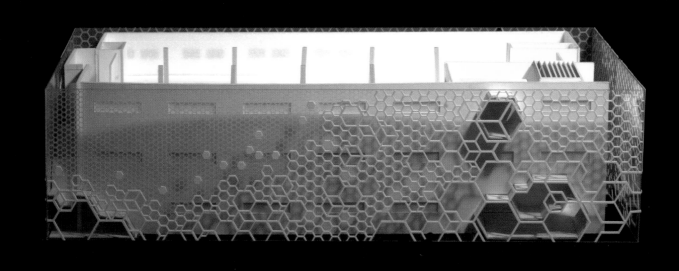

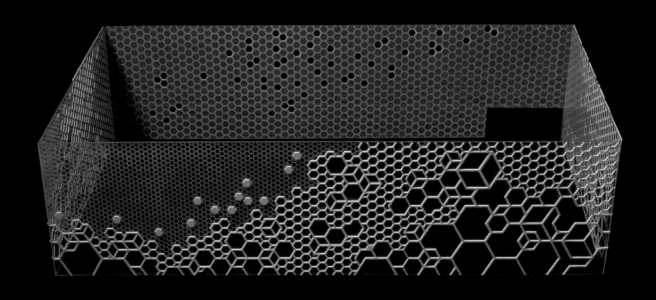

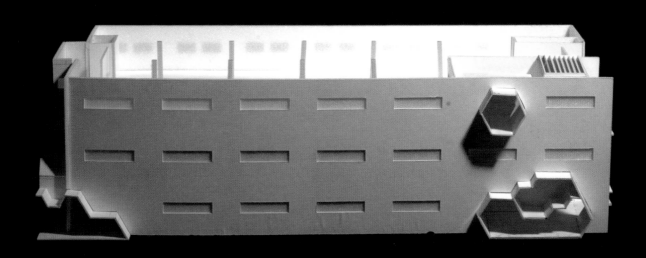

WANG Shu: 'Introverted Vision' and 'Extroverted Vision'

Wang Shu is Dean of the School of Architecture of the China Academy of Art in Zhejiang, but his most important title is that of architectural designer. He designs buildings while he teaches, and his students and fellow teachers work and study in the buildings designed by him. He exercises great influence not only by teaching, but also through his architectural design.

Wang Shu illustrates traditional Chinese spatial aesthetics by pointing to the landscape paintings of the Song Dynasty. The essence of this aesthetic is the relationship between human beings and nature. Building is a platform for people to view nature. With this viewpoint, he develops his ways of observation – 'introverted vision' and 'extroverted vision', which are two different approaches to looking at things.

Located at the eastern side of the mountains of South Hangzhou, the China Academy of Art's Xiangshan Campus (Phases one and two) is Wang Shu's masterwork and established his distinct position as an architectural designer. Phase two is impressive not only in its scope but also in the scale of the buildings. More importantly, Wang Shu has contributed many new building types, which is extremely significant for Chinese architecture. The multiple spatial relationships and the diversity of the buildings are impressive. Moreover, he makes the campus open to the countryside; the dynamic buildings and the waves of the hills reflect each other and the corridors and passages which shuttle between the buildings bring life into the complex.

The double-layered surface of Building Number 15 and the openings on its north elevation are not a formalistic way of showing off, they are rooted in the Chuang Tzu philosophy of 'Musical Aesthetics'. According to this philosophy, it is not necessary to use instruments to discover real music, all one has to do is sit calmly and listen to the wind flowing through the hollows – and in this way hear the most beautiful music in the world.

The rustic style Xiangshan Campus can be understood as a response to the mass demolition and urban regeneration taking place in contemporary China. Over seven million used bricks and tiles of different ages from the entire Zhejiang Province were collected and carried back to the new Xiangshan Campus. The large-scale salvage process expresses the architect's attitude towards society: the recycling of the abandoned materials is not just a matter of environmental or ecological protection, but instead expresses the traditional attitude towards sustainable construction inherent in Chinese culture.

NINGBO ART MUSEUM

LOCATION: **Ningbo, China**
ARCHITECTS: **Wang Shu, Lu Wenyu**
DESIGN COMPANY: **Amateur Architecture Studio**
CORPORATION DESIGN INSTITUTE: **Landscape Design Institute of China Academy of Art**
DESIGN PERIOD: **2001–2002**
CONSTRUCTION PERIOD: **2003–2005**
BUILDING AREA: **about 24,000 m²**
STRUCTURE: **reinforced concrete framework and steel framework**
CLIENT: **Ningbo Art Museum**

P134-P135
1. Elevation of Ningbo Art Museum
   © The Amateur Architecture Studio
2. The huge terrace overlooking the city
   © The Amateur Architecture Studio
3. Bird's-eye view of the Ningbo Art Museum
   © The Amateur Architecture Studio
4. Interior of the exhibition gallery
   © The Amateur Architecture Studio
5. Walkway along the riverside
   © The Amateur Architecture Studio

DESCRIPTION The project is located in the Ningbo Port. The harbour was reconstructed following the removal of its shipping industry to a more rural area. As a part of an overall plan to conserve this historic block, the Amateur Architecture Studio turned what was once the waiting room into a large contemporary art museum. Initially, the plan was to conserve the original building which was built in the 1980s. However, as the construction went on, it was discovered that previous renovations had destroyed certain elements, with the result that the building did not meet the latest architectural regulations. The designer therefore decided to demolish the whole building apart from a beacon tower. The original internal layout, which had long been a part of the city's shared memory, was retained. The building had previously served as the embarkation point for those travelling to Shanghai or making a pilgrimage to the Buddhist holy island of Putuoshan.

The final construction plan contains multiple references in its design. It mirrors the relationship between the port and the ship in its high platform structure and in the shape of the building. Two loading stages are situated in approximately the same place as the disembarkation point. It also reproduces the relationship between the local traditional courtyard buildings and the original building. The museum is accessed from the street via the high platform. Controversially, the building has no magnificent plaza or broad steps, instead the designer has set out to rebuild a Chinese ceremonial space.

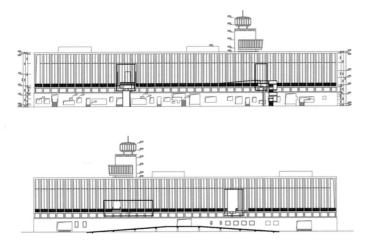

NINGBO HISTORY MUSEUM

LOCATION: **West side of Central Park, Yinzhou District, Ningbo, China**
ARCHITECTS: **Wang Shu, Lu Wenyu**
DESIGN TEAM: **Song Shuhua, Jiang Weihua, Chen Lichao**
DESIGN COMPANY: **Amateur Architecture Studio**
DESIGN PERIOD: **2003–2005**
CONSTRUCTION PERIOD: **2006–2008**
SITE AREA: **45,333 m²**
BUILDING AREA: **30,000 m²**
CLIENT: **Ningbo History Museum**
STRUCTURE: **concrete and steel framework, bridge framework, concrete (internal wall), recycled bricks (external wall)**
MAIN MATERIALS: **bamboo plate model concrete, recycled bricks and tiles, local stone**

DESCRIPTION Until recently a rice field, the site is flat with a view of distant mountains. Urbanization has extended to the area, in which a hundred beautiful villages have been demolished, only one village surviving among the broken tiles. According to the new master plan, buildings must be positioned 100 metres apart from one another, leaving the collapsed structures beyond repair. The question is how to design an isolated object. This building is therefore designed like an artificial mountain, an idea that has roots in the Chinese tradition. But this new mountain doubles as the research centre for an urban topography. The height is limited to 24 metres, arbitrarily defining the cityscape somewhere between the man-made and the natural. Amateur Architecture Studio won an international competition to develop the new museum building.

The lower part of the structure is a simple box. As it rises, the box explodes into the form of a mountain. Visitors enter the museum via an oval cave spanning 30 metres. The internal structure is composed of three valleys with three escalators, one of which is external while the other two connect the interior space. Four caves are arranged at the entrance, the lobby and the cliffs of the exterior valley. Two sunken courtyards dominate the centre and two more discreet ones are hidden further inside. A mountainous topography is superimposed. Multiple routes, rising from ground level up into a labyrinth of pathways, connect the public spaces. This flexible layout is well adapted for the staging of temporary exhibitions. From interior to exterior, the structure is covered with bamboo-cast concrete and more than twenty kinds of recycled bricks and roof tiles. Between the natural and the artificial, provocative yet austere, the structure expresses the raw materials of the mountains. The north wing rests in an artificial lake with reed-covered banks. The water flows over a dam at one end and terminates in a large cobblestone beach. A generous terrace is tucked behind the middle section, with four openings providing views across the city, the rice fields and the distant mountains.

P136-P137
1. The juxtaposition of the tile (Wapian) wall with the bamboo-cast concrete on the east elevation
© The Amateur Architecture Studio
2. Interior view of the atrium
© The Amateur Architecture Studio

P138-P139
1. Detail of the east elevation
© The Amateur Architecture Studio
2. Structure on the roof terrace
© The Amateur Architecture Studio
3. South-west exterior
© The Amateur Architecture Studio
4. Elevation
© The Amateur Architecture Studio
5. Second floor
© The Amateur Architecture Studio

1

①-②Elevation

①-④Elevation

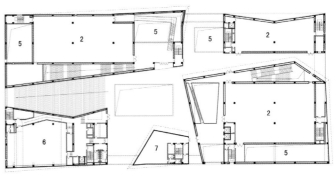

Second floor

XIANGSHAN CAMPUS, CHINA ACADEMY OF ART

LOCATION: **Xiangshan, Zhuangtang, Hangzhou, China**
ARCHITECTS: **Wang Shu, Lu Wenyu**
DESIGN COMPANY: **Amateur Architecture Studio**
CONSTRUCTION PERIOD: **first phase: 2001–2004 / second phase: 2004–2007**
SITE AREA: **266,640 m²**
BUILDING AREA: **about 150,000 m²**
STRUCTURE: **concrete with steel-bar frame and steel in places, brick walls**
MATERIALS: **bamboo planks, concrete, recycled bricks and tiles, local firs and bamboo**

DESCRIPTION Xiangshan Campus is part of the new expansion of the China Academy of Fine Arts to accommodate its School of Architecture, Design, Public Art, Film and Animation, Experiment and Production Centre and Department of Fundamental Teaching. More than 500 staff and 5,000 undergraduate and graduate students study, work and live on this campus.

In 2000, the academy decided to locate its new extension to the east of the South Hangzhou mountains rather than in the popular government-zoned higher education districts. Despite the temporary lack of infrastructure, the academy's professors, artists and architects, all of whom were part of the decision-making process, agreed that according to the Chinese tradition, when it comes to choosing the perfect site for education, the natural landscape is more important than the architecture itself.

The site surrounds a 50-metre hill known as Xiang. Two small brooks from the mountain area in the west run respectively around its north and south sides, merging at the east of the hill before flowing into the Qiantang River. The schematic design of phase one started in 2001 on the north side of the hill and construction finished in 2004. Phase one consists of ten large buildings and two corridors, including the School of Public Art, School of Film and Animation, the library and the gymnasium, a total area of about 70,000 square metres. Phase two started on the south side of the hill in 2004 and was completed in 2007. Ten large buildings and two smaller ones were completed in phase two. These buildings are the School of Architecture, the School of Design, an Experiment and Production Centre, an art museum, another gymnasium, student dormitories and a dining hall.

Historically, traditional Chinese academic buildings were situated in garden courtyards, but the new Xiangshan campus developed a series of topographically different courtyards built in coordination with the hill. The buildings are designed to respond to the contours of the mountains and the rivers. Established farmland, brooks and fishponds are protected. The intricate and poetic spaces of the classic Chinese garden are innovatively transformed into a kind of large-scale pastoral simplicity.

In response to the major programme of demolition and reconstruction in China, more than seven million bricks and roof tiles from across the decades were salvaged from demolition sites all over Zhejiang Province to build the new campus. Reusing, rather than discarding, the bricks and tiles underlines the Chinese vernacular of sustainable construction.

1

3

2

2

3

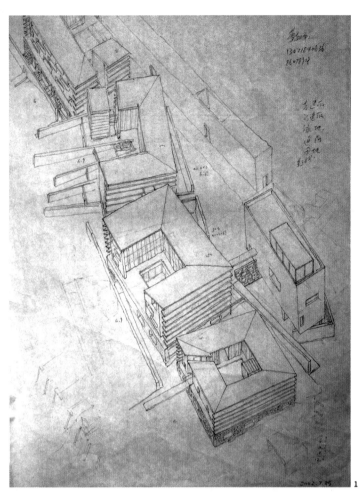

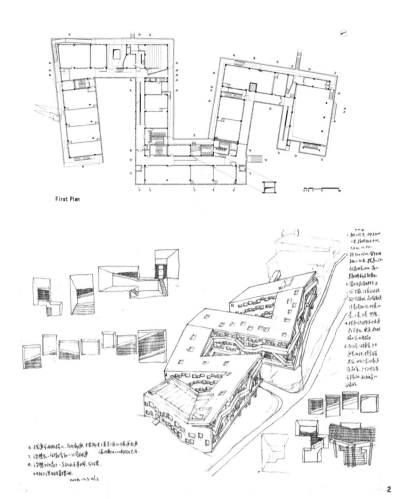

First Plan

WANG Yun: Surrealistic Buildings

Wang Yun is an associate professor at Peking University's Graduate School of Architecture and the chief architect at Atelier Fronti. He has studied both in China and at the University of Tokyo, enabling him to draw upon ideas at the intersection between the study of traditional settlements and the theory and practice of architecture.

In 2002, Wang unveiled his first work since returning to Beijing, '60 Square Metre City', a renovation of his own home based upon his research into settlements and urban spaces, and a visual installation whose elements can trace their lineage back more than a thousand years to organically developed settlements. Wang successfully decoded the symbolism of traditional architecture and translated it into a new contemporary language. Over the past eight years, such symbols have re-emerged and taken on new forms. Whether he is creating designs for houses, schools, kindergartens or government offices, he uses cubes and geometric forms to interpret the world. In his current project, the third phase of the Xixi Wetlands project in Hangzhou, his work recalls the surreal landscapes of the Italian painter Giorgio de Chirico (1888–1978). If completed as planned, it will serve as a compendium of the architectural vocabulary Wang Yun has been exploring over the past few years.

The invitation of Chinese architects to work on projects in the Xixi Wetlands Park has re-shaped the face of the region. Photographs of Xixi show construction across an extensive area. However compelling the reasons for the area's redevelopment, there is a danger that the arrival of developers and architects will lead to the destruction of the wetlands. Natural wetlands are a precious resource for any country and it is our hope that architects will use their work to initiate a dialogue with the surrounding ecosystem.

P146-P147
1. Stairway in the courtyard of Villa A, Lushi Mountain Villas
© Fang Zhenning
2. Courtyard of Villa A at night
© Wang Yun
3. Living room in Villa B
© Fang Zhenning

FINANCIAL TRAINING CENTRE, SHIJINGSHAN DISTRICT

P148-P149
1. View from the west
   © Wang Yun
2. Entrance stairway
   © Wang Yun
3. Close-up view
   © Wang Yun

LOCATION: **Beijing, China**
ARCHITECTS: **Wang Yun / Atelier Fronti**
COLLABORATOR: **M&A Architects and Consultants, International Co. Ltd.**
CONSTRUCTION PERIOD: **2003–2007**
SITE AREA: **9,000 m²**
BUILDING AREA: **7,000 m²**
CLIENT: **Finance Department, Shijingshan District**
USE: **offices**

DESCRIPTION Located on the Fushi Road in the west suburb of Beijing, the building is a block of 40 x 40 x 60 metres containing a grand atrium of 38 x 20 x 20 metres. The building incorporates twenty-three round skylights plus twenty-three circular windows on the west wall. These punched holes introduce the classical Chinese concept of 'chiselling out the door and the window to make a room'.

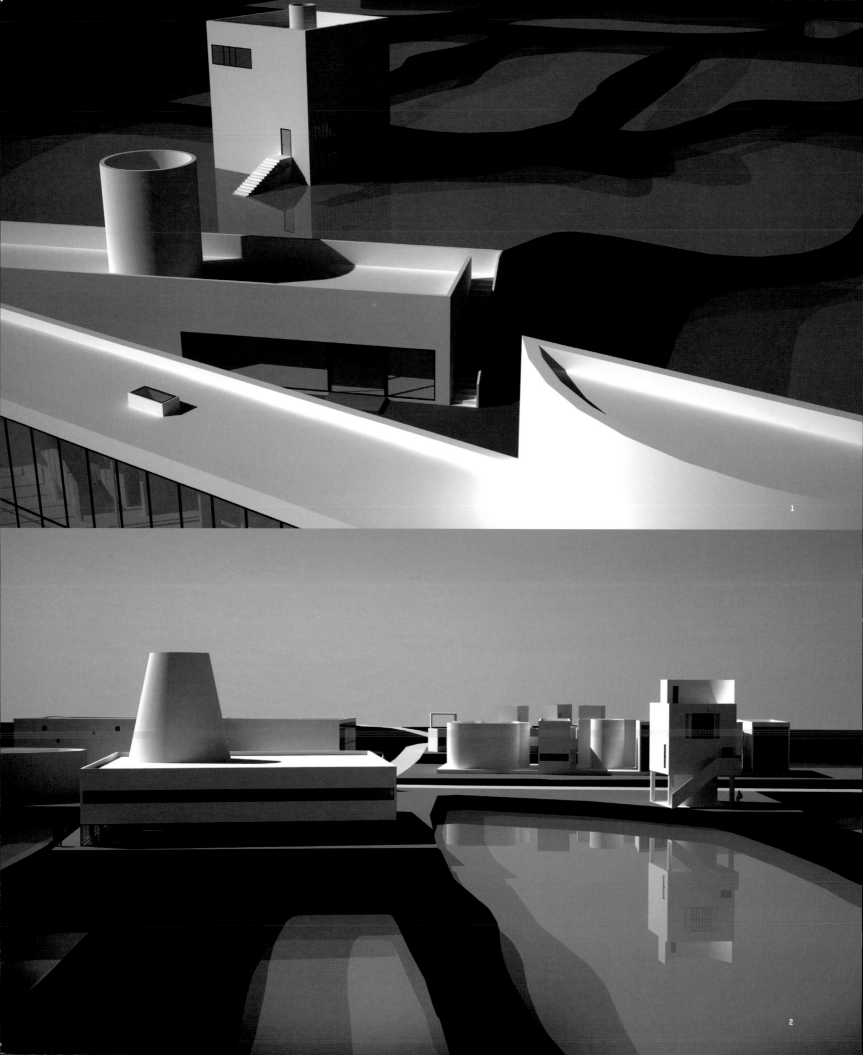

1

2

CLUBHOUSE BUILDINGS

LOCATION: **Hangzhou, China**
ARCHITECTS: **Wang Yun / Atelier Fronti**
PROJECT TEAM: **Atelier Fronti**
COLLABORATOR: **Atelier Fronti + Beijing Zhudufangyuan Architectural Design Co. Ltd.**
CONSTRUCTION PERIOD: **2007–2008**
SITE AREA: **59,802.9 m²**
BUILDING AREA: **3,834.99 m²**
MAIN USE: **clubhouse**

DESCRIPTION This clubhouse design is proposed for the third phase project for the H plot in the Xixi Wetlands Park. Part of the initial concept was to relate the area under construction to the existing natural environment. As a consequence, the overall building scheme is integrated on a single theme encompassing a number of discrete, independent units distributed across the site.

A vital component of traditional Chinese painting is to leave a section of the painting in the original white of the material. Rather than standing for the state of nothingness or insignificance, white produces or stimulates a change in one's emotions and sense of being. It is for this reason that fourteen white buildings were positioned in a nurturing context, which provides both a reflective source and background for the environment as a whole. The harmony between the structures and the surrounding environment creates a unique experience of 'richness in nothingness'.

A combination of geometrical elements has been used to create a sense of coherence. Yet, while the simple geometric forms provide unity, the individual structures within the group are distinguished by small modifications.

P150-P151
1. Detailed computer graphics for A9 building
   © Atelier Fronti
2. Detailed computer graphics of the north buildings
   © Atelier Fronti
3. Master plan
   © Atelier Fronti
4. Detailed computer graphics of the east buildings
   © Atelier Fronti
5. Detailed computer graphics of the north buildings
   © Atelier Fronti

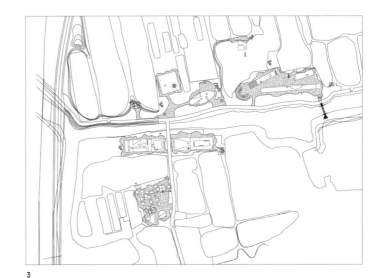

3

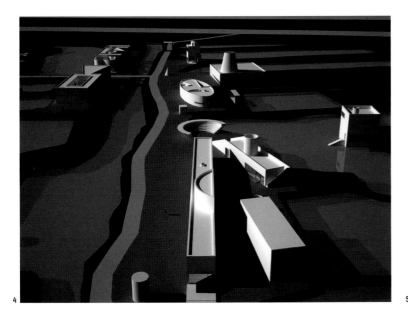

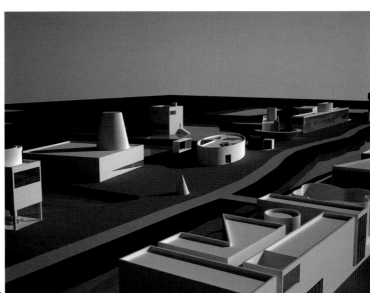

4

5

VILLAS A + B – LUSHI MOUNTAIN VILLAS

LOCATION: **Beijing, China**
ARCHITECTS: **Wang Yun / Atelier Fronti**
PROJECT TEAM: **Atelier Fronti**
COLLABORATOR: **Beijing Xingsheng Architecture & Engineering Design Co. Ltd., Design Department 2**
CONSTRUCTION PERIOD: **2003–2006**
SITE AREA: **A: 688.2 m² / B: 695.6 m²**
BUILDING AREA: **A: 650 m² / B: 640 m²**
CLIENT: **Beijing Jiangong Real Estate**
USE: **housing**

DESCRIPTION The A+B Villas are part of a 57-villa development to the west of Beijing. The two villas are situated side by side, next to the clubhouse, and share a dividing wall. They are arranged across two floors with a full basement. Two courtyards with contrasting atmospheres are placed in the centre. The circulation routes inside each villa allow external views to be incorporated into the overall plan.

P152–P153
1. Bathroom in the basement of Villa A
   © Fang Zhenning
2. West elevation of Villa A at night
   © Fang Zhenning
3. Courtyard of Villa B
   © Fang Zhenning
4. Courtyard of Villa B
   © Fang Zhenning
5. View of the courtyard from Villa B
   © Fang Zhenning

1

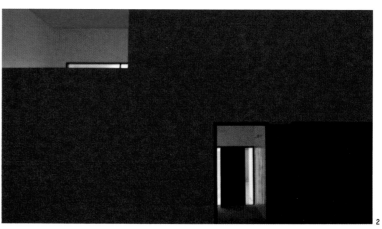

2

3

MIDDLE SCHOOL, BAIZIWAN

LOCATION: **Beijing, China**
ARCHITECTS: **Wang Yun / Atelier Fronti**
PROJECT TEAM: **Atelier Fronti**
COLLABORATOR: **Beijing Xingsheng Architecture & Engineering Design Co. Ltd., Design Department 3**
CONSTRUCTION PERIOD: **2003–2006**
SITE AREA: **25,694 m²**
BUILDING AREA: **11,000 m²**
CLIENT: **Beijing Jiangong Real Estate**
USE: **education**

DESCRIPTION This 24-class middle school is located in the east suburb of Beijing. The three-storey, 157-metre-long rectangular structure has a rectangular courtyard located on the roof of the ground floor. The space is inspired by the underground cave dwellings in the north-west of China.

P154-P155
1. Panoramic view from the south
   © Wang Yun
2. The school courtyard
   © Wang Yun
3. Detail of north elevation
   © Fang Zhenning

1

2

3

KINDERGARTEN, BAIZIWAN

LOCATION: **Beijing, China**
ARCHITECTS: **Wang Yun / Atelier Fronti**
PROJECT TEAM: **Atelier Fronti**
COLLABORATOR: **Beijing Xingsheng Architecture & Engineering Design Co. Ltd., Design Department 3**
CONSTRUCTION PERIOD: **2003–2006**
SITE AREA: **4,009.4 m²**
BUILDING AREA: **3,200 m²**
CLIENT: **Beijing Jiangong Real Estate**
USE: **education**

DESCRIPTION This 3,200 m² three-storey kindergarten is located in the east suburb of Beijing. It is constructed from pure geological elements. The rectangular rooftop courtyard serves both as an outdoor playground and an amphitheatre. The circular courtyard space is used for making music and mirrors the circular music room beneath.

P156-P157
1. Detail of the rooftop amphitheatre
   © Wang Yun
2. View from the northern corridor on the third floor to the rooftop courtyard
   © Wang Yun
3. Detail from the south-east
   © Fang Zhenning
4. South elevation
   © Wang Yun
5. Rooftop amphitheatre
   © Wang Yun

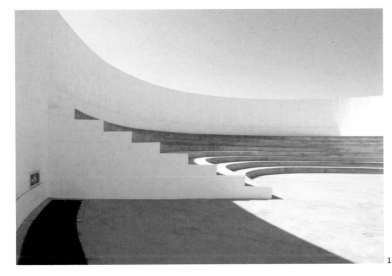

1

2

3

4

5

WANG Dengyue:
Humanism in Architecture

When referring to Chinese contemporary architecture, one's first thought is of the landmark buildings in the main cities. Then there are the so-called experimental buildings. In a country as large as China, it is easy to overlook building projects in the smaller cities. Wang Dengyue is one of those architects whose name is not included in the directory of Chinese architects, but who is serious about producing good design. I got to know his works first from the small project, 'Baohua Chinese Painting Research Institute', and then through a number of completed and uncompleted office building designs.

The 'great leap forward' in China's reconstruction has resulted in many ridiculous and vulgar public buildings, even in the main cities. Wang Dengyue's designs, however, are not ostentatious. He is aware that when undertaking such large-scale reconstruction, if there is no real consideration or restraint, or the buildings do not fully take account of the landscape and environment, it is a disaster for the city.

In the project 'Ningbo North Shore Fortune Plaza', in order to maintain the building's personality and taste, the façade has been designed following strict mathematical modules. The colonnades form appealing shadows in the sunlight and the seamed travertine cladding gives the building a serious aspect. Ningbo North Shore Fortune Plaza is composed of six office buildings arranged at a slight angle to avoid the rigidity of a straight line. Wang Dengyue linked the podium buildings with walkways, uniting the individual blocks. As a whole, the buildings create a sense both of density and lightness. The design of the windows and white walls has taken rhythm into account. Public areas, green spaces and water are particularly important in office buildings, maintaining a fixed but constantly changing relationship with the main buildings. The architect introduced the concepts of people flow and interior high streets into the whole complex, and not only created a strong contrast between the complex commercial space and the rational office façade, but also made the two elements complement each other. The public spaces provide a buffer between the office workers and the commercial flow, while improving the quality of both. In order to maintain the landscaping of Dazha Road, a large sloping lawn was created alongside the street and two-tier commercial facilities were concealed underneath.

Every rooftop of Ningbo North Shore Fortune Plaza is used as green space. Architects often neglect rooftops, and frequently the worst place from which to observe a city is from above, since so many rooftops are covered with equipment or used as storage space. Few consider turning roofs into a garden area or concealing them with an elegant covering.

Wang's talent is also demonstrated in the design of the façades and choice of materials. With these office buildings, his sensitive choices are based on nature, location and landscape while maintaining a minimalist style. He decorated the façades distinctively with glass walls, grey granite and beige travertine cladding.

Fuyang Chinese Painting Research Institute is located in the place depicted in the painting 'Fuchun Mountains' by Huang Gongwang, an artist from the Yuan Dynasty (1269–1354). The region has been home to many famous figures since ancient times. The building area extends across more than 8,000 m², most of which is taken up with exhibition galleries, supplemented by education and research facilities with large studios and living spaces. The grey buildings are covered with greenery. The exhibition areas are divided into upper and lower levels and lit by a crusaders' cross on the top of the gallery cube, allowing natural light to enter the building. The route around the gallery space is carefully designed to ensure that visitors walk counterclockwise without retracing their steps. In order to retain and avoid felling large trees, the architectural layout incorporates them in its design. The hillside building looks like a living organism growing among the trees. Through these details we can see that the designer's humanist sensibility has been poured into this building.

BAOHUA CHINESE PAINTING RESEARCH INSTITUTE

LOCATION: **Fuyang, Zhejiang Province, China**
ARCHITECT: **Wang Dengyue**
CONSTRUCTION PERIOD: **2007**
BUILDING AREA: **8,180 m²**
CLIENT: **Baohua Chinese Painting Research Institute**
USE: **studio, research, exhibitions**

P158-P159
Balcony of the Research Institute
© Fang Zhenning

P160-P161
1. General view
© Wang Dengyue
2. The beautiful landscape surrounding the building
© Fang Zhenning
3. Exterior of the building
© Fang Zhenning
4. The structure is built on a slope
© Fang Zhenning

1

2

ZHU Pei / WU Tong: Non-Architecture has Arrived

It is only a decade since the names of Chinese architects became known on the stage of world architecture and it is only three years since Chinese architects went abroad and took up commissions overseas. Therefore, some of the new names in Chinese architecture are still a little unfamiliar outside China. Zhu Pei is one of these rare and representative architects, although he returned to China from America in 2002. Indeed, there are many Chinese architects who have come back to China from abroad. However, just as it is clear that not everyone who jumps into the sea can swim, it is also evident that only a minority of architects will ever attain great success in a rapidly developing China. Zhu Pei is an outstanding example among the few.

In 2008, the Olympic-related sports buildings became the focal point of architectural interest. Consequently, people have taken less notice of the large-scale Digital Beijing building, erected to the north-west of the Bird's Nest stadium and the Water Cube. The Water Cube's square design provides a sharp but complementary contrast to the circular shape of the Bird's Nest. Similarly, Digital Beijing is made up of four rectangular blocks, strategically situated high above the Bird's Nest and the Water Cube.

Digital Beijing functions as an information control hub and, as such, it requires massive service rooms. Consequently, its appearance is very different from general-purpose office buildings. Inspired by the microchip, its design features vertical lines on its extensive east and west façades. The vertical electronic lines in the east both contrast with and complement the groove design in the west. The enlarged microchip structures and electronic springs both invigorate the rigid walls and enhance the dimensional fluidity. The cyber floating bridge on the ground and lower floors, which gradually extends to take on a curved shape, provides a functional focal point. Both the ground floor and the floating bridge are made of a translucent resin material, creating the impression of being surrounded by a jade forest.

There are no precedents for the designs of Zhu Pei and Wu Tong in traditional architecture. Their works are like functional sculptures or installations and seem to have more in common with modern art than with architecture. From these buildings, it is clear that their design blurs the boundaries between architecture and sculpture, a style that we call by the paradoxical name of 'non-architecture'. It is a style that is only just getting underway.

DIGITAL BEIJING

LOCATION: **Beijing Olympic Park, Beijing, China**
ARCHITECTS: **Zhu Pei, Wu Tong, Wang Hui / Studio Pei-Zhu & Urbanus**
DESIGN TEAM: **Liu Wentian, Lin Lin, Tian Qi, Zeng Xiaoming, He Fan, Li Chun**
STRUCTURAL CONSULTANT: **China Building Standard Design & Research Institute**
CONSTRUCTION PERIOD: **2004–2007**
STRUCTURE AND MATERIALS: **reinforced concrete and steel frame**
BUILDING AREA: **98,000 m²**
CLIENT: **Beijing Network Information Industry Office**
USE: **control and data centre, Beijing Olympics 2008**
AWARD: **international competition prizewinner**

DESCRIPTION The concept for Digital Beijing was developed through a consideration of and reflection on contemporary architecture in the age of digital information. The building emerges from a serene lake like a digital barcode or an integrated circuit board. Here we are seeking a specific form, by attempting to reveal an enlarged micro-world suggestive of microchips, which, although they are so abundant in our daily lives, are usually ignored. With its abstracted mass, like the simple repetition of the digits 0 and 1, this building will be an impressive symbol both of the Digital Olympics and of the information era.

2

3

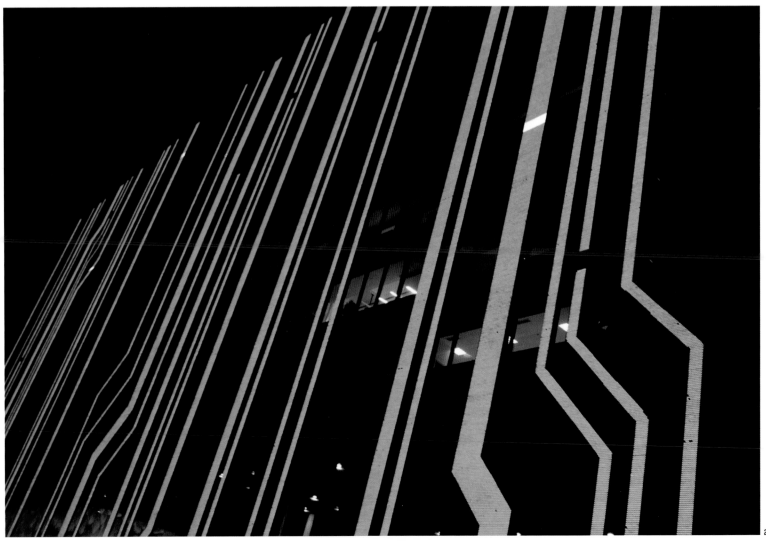

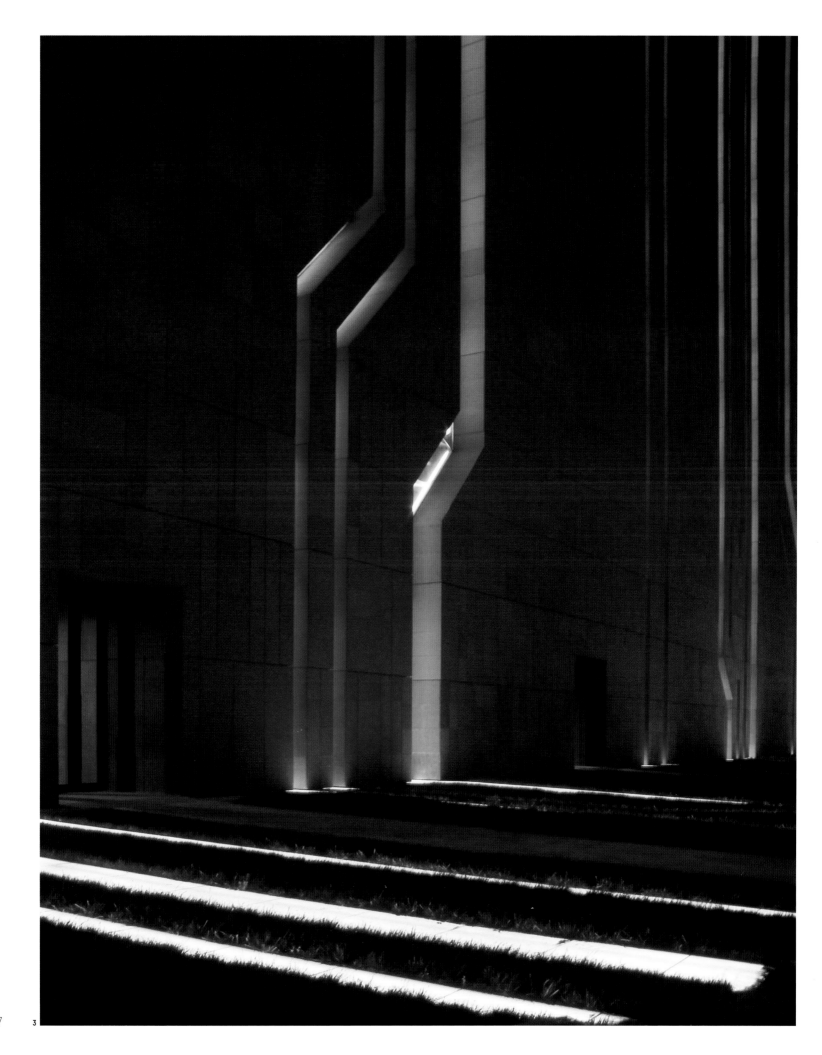

3

BLUR HOTEL

LOCATION: **Beijing, China**
ARCHITECTS: **Zhu Pei, Wu Tong / Studio Pei-Zhu**
DESIGN TEAM: **Li Chun, Zhang Pengpeng, Zhou Lijun, Dai Lili, Wang Min**
ENGINEER: **Beijing Zhongjian Hengji Gongcheng Co. Ltd.**
DESIGN PERIOD: **2004–2005**
CONSTRUCTION PERIOD: **2005–2006**
STRUCTURE AND MATERIALS: **reinforced concrete frame (existing structure) and FRP wall**
BUILDING AREA: **10,176 m²**
CLIENT: **China Resource**
USE: **business hotel and cultural facility**

1

DESCRIPTION The Blur Hotel, located on the site of a large government office beside the western gate of the Forbidden City, is an experiment in 'urban acupuncture'.

As a refurbishment proposal, the project aims to harmonize the existing building with its surroundings and provide a beacon for renewing the area. The first strategy is to open out the ground floor of the building to create a layer of traversable space occupied by public programmes. The second aim is to integrate the building with the local building style, the courtyard house. By carving into the concrete slab floors of the existing building, an arrangement of alternating vertical courtyards is created, replicating the spatial arrangement of the surrounding *hutongs*. The third tactic relates to the exterior of the building, which is wrapped in a continuous and semi-transparent façade. Referring to local traditions, the skin is based on the Chinese lantern. Allowing light to be transmitted both out of and into the building, it turns the building into a single, permeable object.

The façade material used in this project is FRP, a thermosetting plastic that is translucent, rigid and corrosion-resistant. Functionally it is used as a protective surface against the sunlight. On a conceptual level, the extraordinary colour and texture of FRP creates an image of Chinese boulders, generating the translucent glow of a Chinese lantern.

P168-P169
1. The inner courtyard
© Fang Zhenning
2. General view
© Fang Zhenning
3. Central courtyard
© Fang Zhenning

CAI GUO-QIANG COURTYARD HOUSE RENOVATION

LOCATION: **Beijing, China**
ARCHITECTS: **Zhu Pei, Wu Tong / Studio Pei-Zhu**
PROJECT TEAM: **Liu Wentian, Hao Xiangru, Li Shaohua, He Fan**
STRUCTURAL CONSULTANT: **Xu Minsheng**
CONSTRUCTION PERIOD: **2006–2007**
SITE AREA: **910.33 m²**
BUILDING AREA: **412.72 m²**
CLIENT: **Cai Guo-Qiang**
USE: **private housing**

DESCRIPTION 'Reinforce the old, introduce the new' is the theme of this design. The original architecture has been well respected and preserved. The house functions as a memory stick, recording every trace that history has left on it. The new addition, with its titanium-aluminum alloy metal façade, expresses a futuristic notion. The combination of modern Beijing together with the old house creates a dialogue between the old and the new. The three compartments that form the two courtyards have been given three spatial themes. The northern section was defined as 'three-dimensional installation'. The old wood structure in this room was exposed to emphasize its strength. The middle section was defined as 'two-dimensional Chinese painting' – white walls dominate the interior, creating a feeling of relaxation and grace. The southern section was defined as 'futuristic space'. The old and new architecture both contrast and communicate with each other. The visual and spatial links between the courtyards form a symphony between tradition and the future.

P170-P171
1. Computer image: bird's-eye-view
   © Studio Pei-Zhu
2. Tea-room, after renovation
   © Fang Zhenning

P172-P173
1. Corridor, after renovation
   © Fang Zhenning
2. Courtyard after renovation
   © Studio Pei-Zhu
3. Detail, after renovation
   © Fang Zhenning
4. Detail, after renovation
   © Fang Zhenning
5. North courtyard view from the living room,
   after renovation
   © Fang Zhenning
6. Plan
   © Studio Pei-Zhu

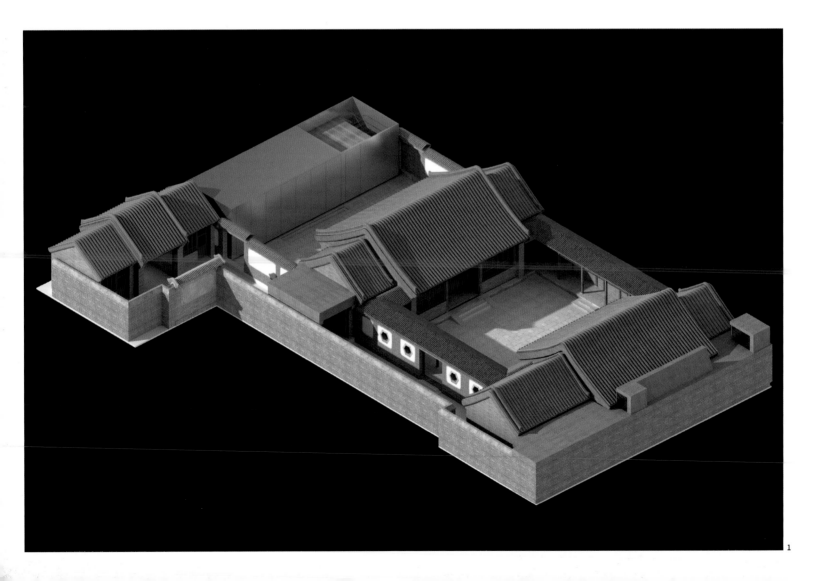

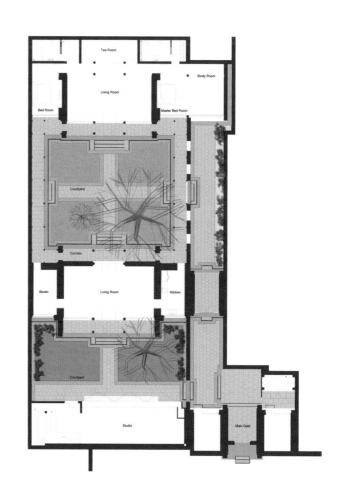

ZHUANG Weimin:
Design Reliant on Nature

Chinese civilization has its roots in nature, when all human activity revolved around the availability of natural light, the direction of the wind and other natural phenomena. One of the philosophies behind the 2008 Beijing Olympic Games was that it should be a 'green' Olympics. The Judo and Taekwondo Gymnasium for the Beijing Olympic Games, located in the Beijing Science and Technology University, uses a device known as a 'light pipe' that absorbs natural daylight to produce a green lighting system.

The chief designer of the Judo and Taekwondo Gymnasium was Dr Zhuang Weimin from the Architectural Design and Research Institute of Tsinghua University. Bearing in mind the special requirements of the gym, he adopted the 'light pipe' illumination system. This works by the use of high-performance light-absorbing shades which collect and redistribute natural light into the lighting system. After being transmitted and intensified by specially made light pipes, a diffusion apparatus at the base of the system directs the natural light to the desired locations uniformly and efficiently. This system consists of three main parts: light absorbers, light conductors and light diffusers. The indoor illumination provided by this system is sufficient to light the building from dawn to dusk, even on cloudy and rainy days. However, the technology opens up possibilities and applications beyond its use in the Olympics gymnasia. Compared to conventional illumination systems, light pipe illumination has the advantage of being entirely green, as it has a neutral impact on the environment and consumes no energy, subsequently it has been heralded with enthusiasm both in China and abroad.

The energy-saving light pipe illumination system can be used to replace electrical light during the daytime, since it is capable of providing at least ten hours of natural lighting a day. The light is diffused and uniform, so cannot be compared with any other type of artificial light. In addition, the system has no safety problems, since it does not require any electrical equipment or wires, thereby eradicating the danger of fire caused by deteriorating wires.

P174-P175
1. Light pipe diffuser and cokuloris
© Architectural Design & Research Institute of Tsinghua University
2. Light pipe diffuser
© Architectural Design & Research Institute of Tsinghua University

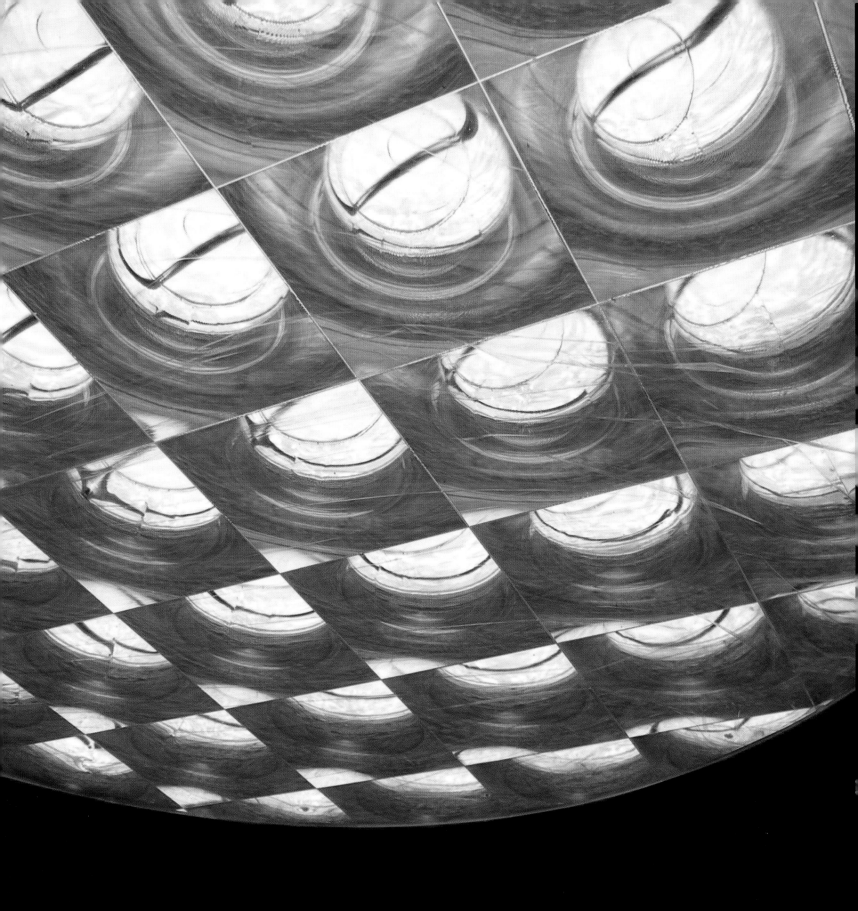

BEIJING SCIENCE AND TECHNOLOGY UNIVERSITY GYMNASIUM (JUDO AND TAEKWONDO GYMNASIUM FOR THE 2008 BEIJING OLYMPIC GAMES)

LOCATION: **Beijing Science and Technology University, Haidian District, Beijing, China**
ARCHITECT: **Zhuang Weimin**
STRUCTURAL ENGINEERING: **Architectural Design and Research Institute, Tsinghua University**
CONSTRUCTION PERIOD: **2006–2008**
SITE AREA: **23,800 m²**
BUILDING AREA: **24,662.32 m²**
CLIENT: **Beijing Science and Technology University**
USE: **2008 Beijing Olympics gymnasium and university gymnasium**

DESCRIPTION The light pipe illumination system adopted here is well suited to the needs of the Judo and Taekwondo Gymnasium, and it embodies the first of the three main philosophies of the Beijing Olympics: 'Green Olympics, Humanistic Olympics and Technical Olympics.' It works through high-performing light absorption shades that collect and introduce natural light into the illumination system for re-distribution. After being transmitted and intensified by specially made light pipes, natural light is directed to the desired locations uniformly and efficiently by a diffusion apparatus at the bottom of the system. The indoor illumination provided by this system is sufficient from dawn to dusk, even on cloudy or rainy days. It consists of three parts: light absorbing, light conducting and diffusion apparatus.

In this gym, 148 light pipes (530 mm in diameter and with an index of refraction of 99.7%) have been installed, making it the building with the highest number of light pipes in China. With adequate sunshine, the light collected is able to satisfy sports requirements, without the need for electrical lights, or only a few at the most. The light pipes, while transmitting sunshine into the gym during the daytime, can also be used to transmit indoor light out through the light-absorbing shades during the night, enhancing the nocturnal landscape.

P176-P177
1. The light receiver for the 148 light pipes on the roof
© Architectural Design & Research Institute of Tsinghua University
2. West elevation of Judo and Taekwondo Gymnasium
© Architectural Design & Research Institute of Tsinghua University
3. Bird's-eye view of Judo and Taekwondo Gymnasium
© Architectural Design & Research Institute of Tsinghua University

3

HOLL Steven / LI Hu: Continuous Creativity

Over the last ten years, many Western architects have joined the rapidly expanding wave of construction that is taking place in China. Few of them, however, are in a position to settle there permanently, making it extremely difficult both to secure projects and to work on them without interruption. As might be expected, some of the established world-class architects who wanted to be a part of the Beijing Olympic Games went away disappointed. Nevertheless, other architects, particularly those who pay close attention to the use and development of sustainable resources, are more than willing to experiment in China.

Steven Holl is one example of an American architect who holds China in great esteem. He rose to fame with his design for the Linked Hybrid complex in Beijing. In March 2008, when I first saw his design for the Sliced Porosity Block on the internet, I immediately expressed my admiration for it in my blog: 'Without doubt, Steven Holl will become the most popular architect after Koolhaas. He neither repeats himself nor does he repeat the work of other people. At a time when many star architects' creativity is in decline, Holl's is increasing.'

Holl comments, 'I choose to work in China, mainly because I can look into and learn more about architecture in the twenty-first century, for example, building a sustainable resource system and a comprehensive city.' He also remarks, 'American property developers should come to see how the sustainable resource system is carried out here in China.' It is hard to say exactly how Holl secures his contracts so easily; maybe it is because he shows such a high regard for local feng shui, or perhaps the Chinese have changed their taste. However, he is evidently committed to the design of eco-architecture. The Sliced Porosity Block, though not yet completed, has gained the precertification of the LEED (Leadership in Energy and Environmental Design) gold rating awarded by the USGBC (US Green Building Council). This complex will be heated and cooled geo-thermally and it will incorporate a wide range of heat-recycling equipment as well as cold and hot water storage and a system for recycling and reusing water. It will also have abundant greenery on roofs and podium buildings, take advantage of regional materials, make use of solar energy and generally adopt other environmentally-friendly measures. The Vanke Centre, Shenzhen, another eco-friendly building that is currently under construction, was also designed by Holl.

Although Holl took up architecture very late – he previously worked as a teacher – in 1993 he won the design competition for the Helsinki Contemporary Art Museum in Finland. He lives like an artist: every morning he drinks a cup of coffee and produces a watercolour of a piece of architecture, rather like doing exercises. That is why Holl's designs are so varied and imaginative. His expression and inspiration emanate from this traditional practice. Holl has the essential quality for an architect: the ability to be continuously creative.

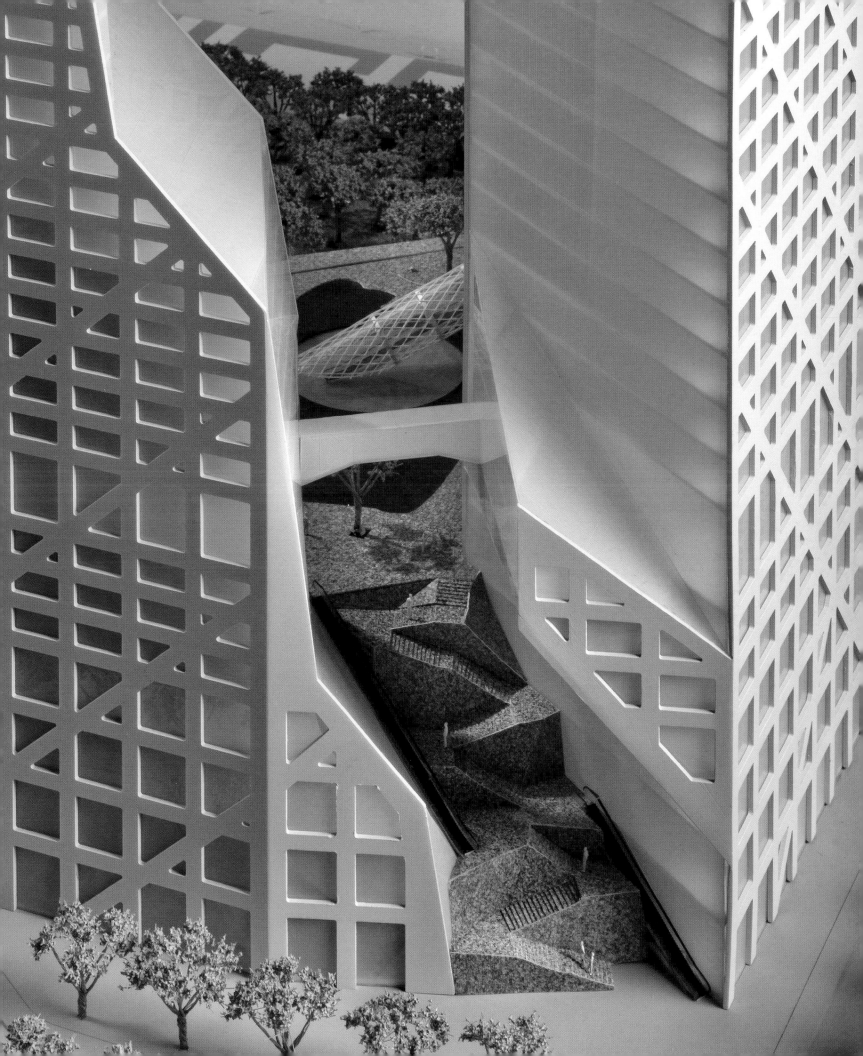

VANKE CENTRE

LOCATION: **Shenzhen, China**
ARCHITECTS: **Steven Holl, Li Hu**
PROJECT TEAM: **Steven Holl, Li Hu, Yimei Chan, Gong Dong, Garrick Ambrose (SD/DD), Maren Koehler (DD), Jay Siebenmorgen (DD), Christopher Brokaw, Rodolfo Dias (CD), Eric Li, Jason Anderson, Guanlan Cao, Lesley Chang, Clemence Eliard, Forrest Fulton, Nick Gelpi, M. Emran Hossain, Seung Hyun Kang, JongSeo Lee, Wan-Jen Lin, Richard Liu, Jackie Luk, Enrique Moya-Angeler, Roberto Requejo, Jiangtao Shen, Michael Rusch, Filipe Taboada, Justin Allen, Johnna Brazier, Kefei Cai, Yenling Chen, Hideki Hirahara**
CONSTRUCTION PERIOD: **2006–**
SITE AREA: **1,204,449 m²**
CLIENT: **Shenzhen Vanke Real Estate Co. Ltd.**
USE: **hotel, offices, condominiums, public park**

DESCRIPTION Hovering over a tropical garden, this 'horizontal sky-scraper' – as long as the Empire State Building is tall – unites into one vision the headquarters for Vanke Co. Ltd., office spaces, apartments and a hotel. A conference centre, spa and parking are located under the large green public landscape.

The building looks as though it once floated on a higher sea that has now subsided, leaving the structure propped up on eight legs. The decision to float one large structure below the 35-metre height limit, instead of building several smaller structures each catering to a specific requirement, was inspired by the desire to create views across the lower developments of surrounding sites to the South China Sea and to generate the largest possible public green space at ground level.

The underside of the floating structure becomes its main elevation from which sunken glass cubes, the so-called 'Shenzhen Windows', offer 360-degree views across the lush tropical landscape below. A public pathway, running along the entire length of the building, has been designed to connect the hotel, the apartment zones and the office wings.

The floating horizontal building allows sea and land breezes to pass through the public gardens. The landscape, inspired by Roberto Burle Marx's gardens in Brazil, incorporates restaurants and cafés in verdant mounds flanked by pools and walkways. At night, a walk through this landscape of flowering tropical plants will be enhanced by the smell of jasmine and the colourful glow of the undersides of the structure floating above.

As a tropical, sustainable twenty-first-century vision, the building and the landscape integrate several new sustainable aspects. The Vanke Headquarters wing of the floating horizontal skyscraper is aiming for a LEED Platinum rating for its environmentally sustainable construction. The Vanke Centre is a tsunami-proof hovering architecture that creates a porous microclimate for the landscapes beneath.

P180-P181
1. The upper building hovers over the landscape
© Eric Li / Steven Holl Architects
2. The building's double skin with aluminium louvre shading system
© Eric Li / Steven Holl Architects

P182-P183
1. The upper building
© Eric Li / Steven Holl Architects
2. Vanke Centre under construction; expected completion date autumn 2009
© Eric Li / Steven Holl Architects
3. Balconies at each end provide excellent views towards the sea
© Eric Li / Steven Holl Architects

1

SLICED POROSITY BLOCK

LOCATION: **Chengdu, China**
ARCHITECTS: **Steven Holl, Li Hu**
PROJECT TEAM: **Steven Holl, Li Hu, Roberto Bannura, Lan Wu, Haiko Cornelissen, JongSeo Lee, Christiane Deptolla, Inge Goudsmit, Maki Matsubayashi, Sarah Nichols, Martin Zimmerli, Justin Allen, Jason Anderson, Francesco Bartolozzi, Yimei Chan, Sofie Holm Christensen, Peter Englaender, Esin Erez, Ayat Fadaifard, Mingcheng Fu, Forrest Fulton, Runar Halldorsson, M. Emran Hossain, Joseph Kan, Suping Li, Tz-Li Lin, Jackie Luk, Daijiro Nakayama, Pietro Peyron, Roberto Requejo, Elena Rojas-Danielsen, Ida Sze, Filipe Taboada, Human Wu**
CONSTRUCTION PERIOD: **2007–2010**
BUILDING AREA: **3,120,000 m²**
CLIENT: **CapitaLand Development**
USE: **five towers with offices, serviced apartments, retail, hotel, cafés, restaurants**

DESCRIPTION Steven Holl Architects (SHA) has recently been commissioned by CapitaLand China to realize a large mixed-use complex in Chengdu, China. Scheduled to open in late 2010, this 'giant chunk of a metropolis' houses a hybrid complex of generous public spaces flanked by five towers with offices, serviced apartments, retail, a hotel, cafés and restaurants. The huge site is developed to maximize public open space and to stimulate micro-urbanism.

The 'Sliced Porosity Block' will be located just south of the intersection of the First Ring Road and Ren Min Nan Road. Its sun-sliced geometry results from minimum daylight exposures to the surrounding urban fabric as prescribed by local building regulations. Porous and inviting from every side, five vertical entrances cut through a layer of micro-urban shopping before leading to the elevated public 'Three Valley' plaza. A great urban terrace on the scale of New York's Rockefeller Centre, this multi-level plaza in the centre of the complex is sculpted by stone steps, ramps, trees and ponds, and caters for special events or simply a casual afternoon in the sun. Here, the public space parallax of overlapping geometries in strict black and white is supercharged by colour that glows from the shops positioned underneath the plaza.

The three generous ponds on the plaza, which 'Time has left stranded in Three Valleys', are inspired by the poem by Du Fu (AD 713–770), one of ancient China's most important poets, who spent a part of his life in Chengdu. These three ponds function as skylights to the six-storey shopping precinct beneath, and are pierced by diagonal stray escalators that thrust upwards to three 'buildings within buildings'. Residing on voids in the façades of the sculpted blocks these pavilions are

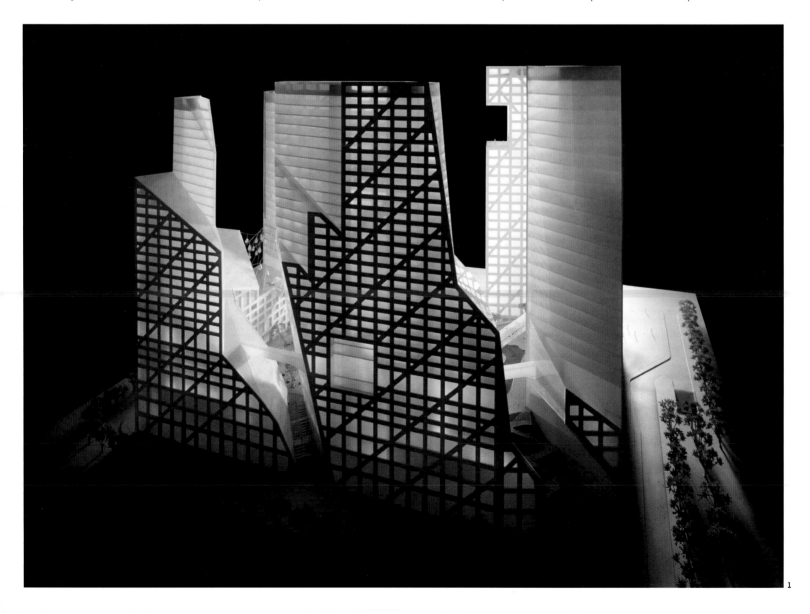

the History Pavilion (designed by Steven Holl), the High-tech Pavilion (designed by Lebbeus Woods) and the Du Fu Pavilion.

The 'Sliced Porosity Block' is heated and cooled geo-thermally and the large ponds in the plaza harvest recycled rainwater while the natural grasses and lily pads create a natural cooling effect. High-performance glazing, energy-efficient equipment and the use of regional materials are just a few of the other features employed to reach the LEED gold rating.

P184-P185
1. Sliced Porosity Block viewed from the east with hotel and serviced apartment towers in the foreground
   © Iwan Bann
2. Du Fu Pavilion and plaza upper levels can be seen through the visual corridors that also function as plaza entry points
   © Iwan Bann
3. An important contribution to the city: the plaza merges with the urban space and activities of Ren Min Nan Road, as viewed from the street's southern approach
   © Iwan Bann·

P186-P187
   The concrete frame and curtain wall complement each other, accentuating the 'sun slices' in the block
   © Iwan Bann

2

3

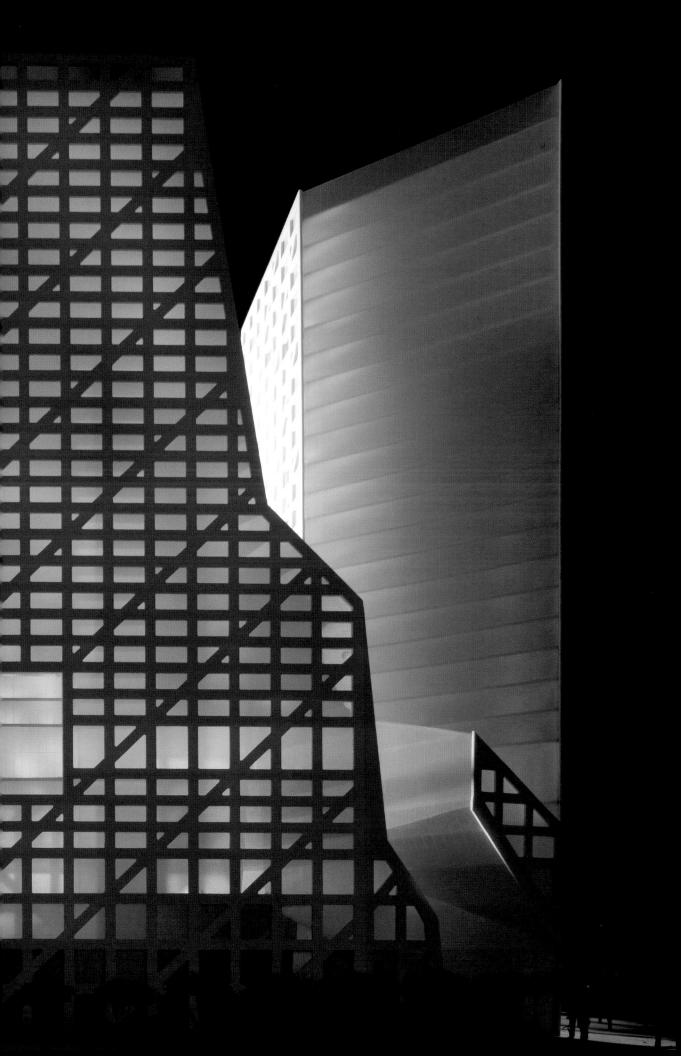

DIGITAL ARCHITECTURE

CHEN Yuanyuan

FENG Shuai

CHEN Yuanyuan:
Future Marine City

If Chen Yuanyuan's 'Future Marine City' gives the impression of a Utopia, one need look no further than her design background and choice of project for confirmation. Her selection of 'Future Marine City' as the theme for her graduate work reveals the bold new vision of China's younger architects for the future – not merely challenging or mocking history, but envisioning a future from a purely architectural perspective.

On 12 January 2008, the city of Shanghai announced an ecotypic planning research topic named 'Marine City', with the goal of constructing an environmentally sustainable offshore city developed through a series of five-year plans. An area 6.5 km² on the north side of Hangzhou Bay was preliminarily selected for the site, which was to support a population of 50,000 to 80,000 people. It was the announcement of this project that set Chen Yuanyuan's mind to work.

One might imagine a complex on the sea, with vertical structures capable of housing about a thousand residents: a rational design and good functionality and, as well as the high rises, schools, sports fields, parks, shopping malls, docks and cultural centres. One might decide to use the underwater area for office space and non-harmful industrial plants to satisfy the city's need for industry. This plan would use a network of above-water corridors, underwater tunnels and vertical elevators, with each network connecting to more casual spaces as well as housing commercial, office and residential areas.

Chen Yuanyuan, however, took her inspiration from the womb and from coral reefs, using models to simulate the organic, biological processes that make up a city. In Chen's vision, an observer looking at this marine city from the land or at a distance across the water would see buildings surrounded by the ocean – a sight of paternal solemnity. Upon entering the city, however, people would feel a motherly warmth and security.

In Chen's vision, marine megastructures will provide residential centres for people as the largest and most vibrant spaces. We may explore the feasibility of such structures by considering organic forms. The 'megastructures' of Chen's plan refer to high-density, finely integrated systems forming a continuous, flexible structure capable of sustaining natural life. Chen designed her marine structures as polygonal meshes after taking inspiration from cellular structures. Like living, breathing things, these structures appear to be a unitary whole from outside, but inside they are richly complex.

Chen believes that future megastructures will follow the evolution of human culture and the progress of human society and will, in the form of massive human dwelling spaces, continue to evolve and expand. 'In every age,' she says, 'the future of architecture has always been a dream that will come true.'

MIRAGE – FUTURE MARINE CITY

LOCATION: **Hangzhou Bay, China**
ARCHITECT: **Chen Yuanyuan**
USE: **housing, offices, entertainment**

DESCRIPTION With the evolution of civilization and social development, 'megastructure' – an advanced form of human communal living – will continuously emerge, extend, mature and die. It can protect the fragile human being because, in future hostile environments, people will need not only the expansion and variation of space, but also the sense of security they once felt in the warmth of the womb.

This marine city will be a future centre of human settlement, which can accommodate tens of thousands of people, even reaching the scale of a medium-sized city. It imitates the configuration and regular growth of the bio-organism. Its human-scaled cell body serves as the basic spatial unit, with a polygonal lattice acting as the supporting system enclosing a super-scaled public area.

P189
   Mirage – Future Marine City (detail)
   © Chen Yuanyuan

P190-P191
   Architectural design
   © Chen Yuanyuan

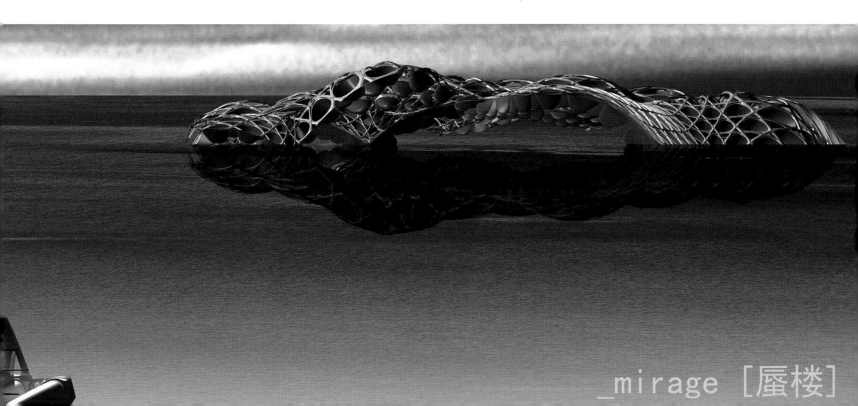

_mirage [蜃楼]

FENG Shuai: Emergent Designs

Feng Shuai graduated from China's Central Academy of Fine Arts in 2008 and is now doing a master's degree at the Architectural Association School of Architecture in London. He was honoured with a distinction in his graduate study and is one of China's young generation of digital architects. His final thesis project on the National Museum building in Tiananmen Square is both original and creative in its design.

In the past, architecture responded with great sophistication and beauty to the need to preserve local resources and provide diverse and suitable conditions for human habitation. Feng Shuai studied the acoustic performance of the spiral ceiling topology, a form that is widespread in the Jiangnan region of China. This method has long been considered to be effective in preventing the dispersal and absorption of sound in opera stages. However, recent studies show that it has the opposite effect: of absorption instead of deflection. This effect is useful in halls with large spaces in which the sound needs to be deflected. The ceiling structure required for this acoustic arrangement is complex, although it is based on a simple repeating formula. In order to generate the morphology to a complex level, a flocking algorithm was used to simulate artificial intelligence swarming behaviours.

Emergence has become an important concept in biology and mathematics, artificial intelligence, information technology and computer science, as well as in the newer domains of weather and climate studies and material sciences. Commonplace terms such as 'self-organizing structures' and 'bottom-up systems' have their origin in the science of emergence.

Computers work by producing complex results from numerous simple changes. References from 'ant fugue' in Douglas Hofstadter's book, *Godel, Escher, Bach: An Eternal Golden Braid*, have enlightened our understanding of the nature of computation. A single ant might be simple, with a limited capacity for logic at an elementary level, but when it is part of a colony, new kinds of higher intelligence emerge.

In his final project, Feng Shuai used clamps to represent a matrix of components, after which a vector system was used to control the overall behaviour. Through the Japanese junctions of each component, which possesses its flexibility response to vibrancy, it could be observed that the vector matrix has an adaptation to each direction around the centre of the circle. While it is a swarming adaptive system, Feng Shuai found his inspiration in the intelligence of the past.

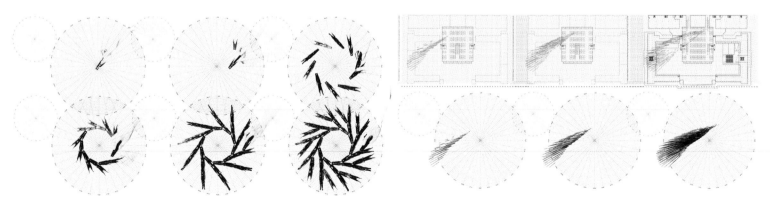

EMERGENT TECHNOLOGIES IN NATIONAL MUSEUM DESIGN

LOCATION: **Tiananmen Square, Beijing, China**
ARCHITECT: **Feng Shuai**
USE: **architectural design**

DESCRIPTION The proposal for the new National Museum basically dealt with the enclosure of the main courtyard. After the analysis of the traditional spiral ceiling construction, which has long existed in the southern regions of China, it was concluded that the spiral ceiling could be improved.

To improve acoustics in a large-scale space, while avoiding sound pollution, parametric technologies were introduced to locate the direction of the ceiling components. In addition, an adaptability was achieved both in horizontal and vertical level through the junctions of flexibility.

P192-P193
1. Conceptual diagram
   © Feng Shuai
2. Detail
   © Feng Shuai
3. Detail
   © Feng Shuai
4. Detail
   © Feng Shuai

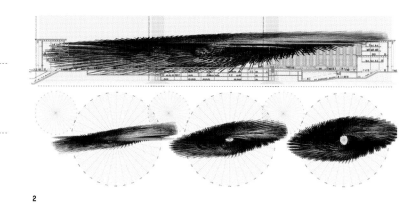

2

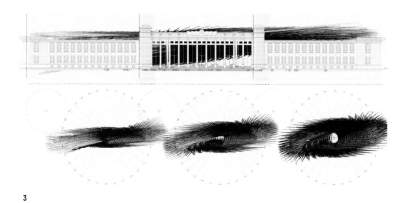

3

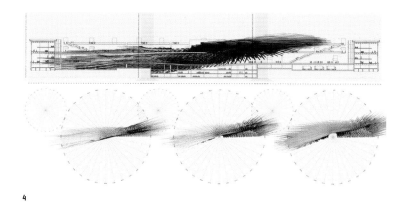

4

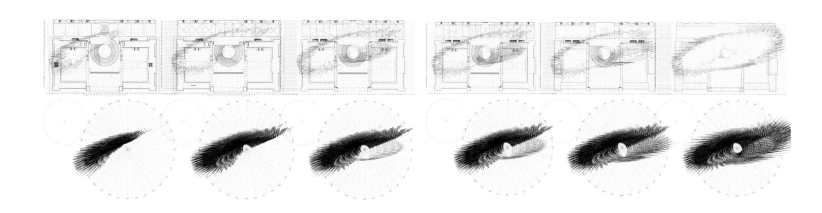

VIDEO ARCHITECTURE

WANG Di

XIAO Wei

ZHANG Xiaotao

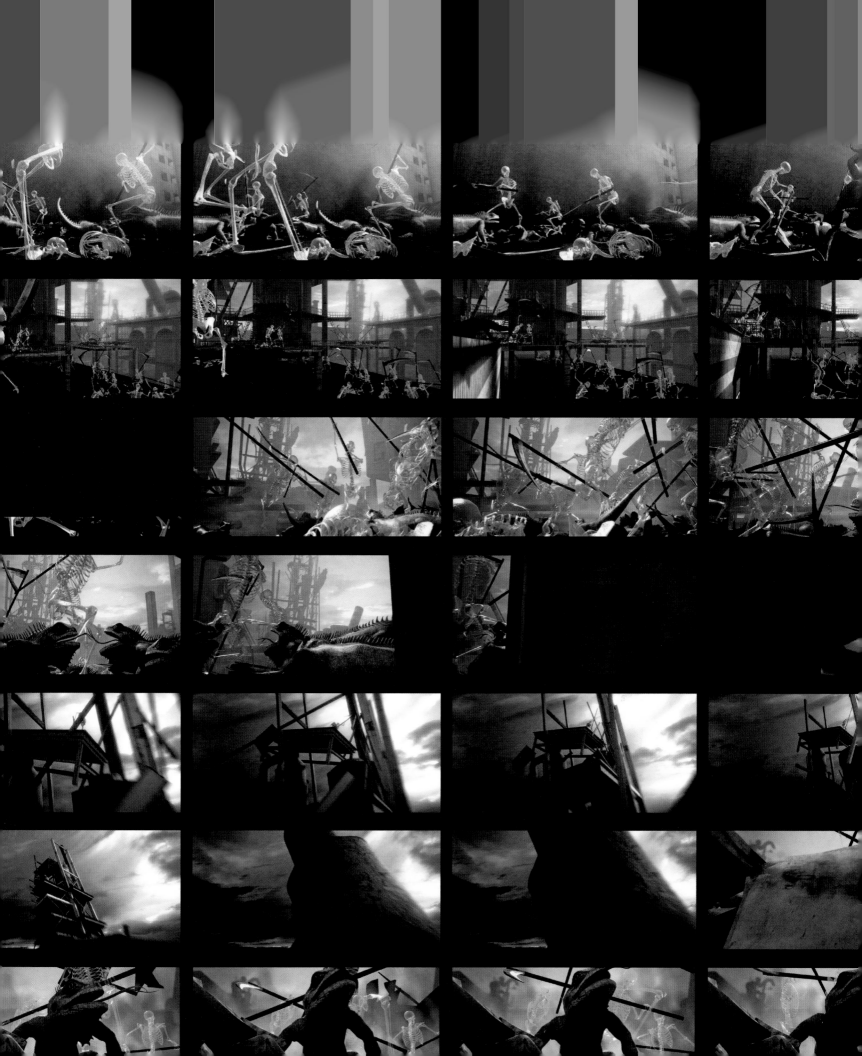

WANG Di:
Naturally Growing Streets

Wang Di's photo-scroll, 'Growth – Beijing Streets', reveals the charm of ordinary Chinese architecture and streets. Though there are not many true *hutongs* (traditional alleyways) left in Beijing, daily life continues in the *hutong* areas of the city much as it always has. Photography is a documentary art, but Wang combined his photographs together into a long scroll – to provide subjective observations that the viewer would not have arrived at with a purely objective eye. The streets in Wang's photographs are contrasting imprints left upon the city by the various ages through which it has existed. His pictures are a meditation upon the natural relationship of growth – and unnatural destruction – between urban architecture and its environment.

Beijing, though an ancient city that has known several dynasties, was planned rather than growing as organic development. A closer look at Wang's photographs, however, reveals centuries of cultural transmission, of add-ons and expansions made by successive generations of residents and the natural emergence of the grassroots culture and the beating heart that still make Beijing the city it is. Over the past century, however, the destruction of the chain of cultural transmission and clashes between new and old cultures and concepts have left scars on the city that cannot heal. To capture his images in as realistic and detailed a fashion as possible, 'Beijing Streets' uses 8 x 10 photographic prints, with the final work comprising thirty-five 8 x 10 images.

Wang Di has long been an artist concerned with the city. In his series 'Our Things: Red Houses' he turned his lens on the red houses built in Beijing during the 1950s and 1960s as a means of showing the changes that have reshaped the city. Wang chose a number of representative old buildings from around the city that, whether pristine, tumbledown or – in many cases – largely demolished, still reflect the living memories of Beijing in the rays of the rising and setting sun.

GROWTH – BEIJING STREETS 2008

ARTIST: **Wang Di**
PRODUCED: **2008**
CATEGORY: **Photography**
FORMAT: **photo-scroll**
MATERIALS: **8 x 10 camera, 8 x 10 film**
Copyright © Wang Di

DESCRIPTION The photographs in 'Growth – Beijing Streets' are an interpretation of the theme 'ordinary architecture'. I tried to show the conflict between the natural 'growing' and 'non-growing' relationship between architecture and the environment through continuous shooting of several *hutong* (traditional alleyway) blocks in Beijing. As the capital of various dynasties, the city of Beijing was realized in a top-down manner rather than spontaneously spawned as one from the very beginning. Nevertheless, if you look at the details, you will see how the cultural tradition of hundreds of years and the citizens' constant improvements in living conditions and culture have

produced a subtle and continuous urban fabric. In the past 100 years, however, the breakdown of that tradition and the clashing of old and new cultures and ideologies have resulted in a lot of incongruity and the discontinuity of what we call the 'growing relationship'. It is this condition on which 'Growth – Beijing Streets' is focused.

XIAO Wei: New Way / New Relation

The 'SelfVoice' video programme (2007–2009) is the first exhibit by cutting-edge video artist Xiao Wei.

'SelfVoice' is a video exchange programme that encourages participants to ask a question and then answer it themselves. It aims to create a new context of self-reflection and expression, facilitating a potential interaction between participants and observers, which is a new approach in video art. Xiao Wei's role is intentionally ambiguous; she is the founder of the programme, acting as the director, operating and manipulating the entire project, but she doesn't appear in the film. All the videos presented to the audience/observers have only been slightly edited. Basically, Xiao Wei hides herself behind the scenes to maximize the retention of the entire 'self-voice' process.

The objectivity of documentary films has constantly been questioned. It has been stated that as long as a cameraman is holding the camera, a degree of subjectivity is involved. And this is an embarrassing question for almost all the documentary directors. By contrast, Xiao Wei chooses a new approach and 'SelfVoice' is a new video concept rather than a documentary.

'SelfVoice' is composed of a series of videos with each video containing three questions asked and responded to by the participant. It is a self-dialogue, an integrated statement and an uninterrupted contemplation. The additional information conveyed by the video, as well as the self-communication tool, introduces a complete context with more descriptive language information for the interaction between participants and their questions. From Xiao Wei's point of view, there is no direct contact between this self-communication and observers but, to some extent, it is much like the way we live today. Many of us live in different 'boxes' in high-rise apartments, with little interaction even between others on the same floor; instead, interaction happens in digital spaces, websites / chat rooms / online-games / instant messaging and so on. The digital space is not reality, but virtual reality bears some similarity, keeping this impact in our daily life. Traditional face-to-face communication has been transformed into a complex (multi-)digital space, with a degree of self-expression and mutual peeping.

如何的在现实世界之间进行展示
how to present in real world

1

就是好的房子它似乎并不是一个陌生的东西
a good architecture is probably not strange for us

2

SELFVOICE

ARTIST: **Xiao Wei**
PRODUCED: **2009**
CATEGORY: **interactive documentary**
Copyright © Xiao Wei

DESCRIPTION 'SelfVoice' is a video exchange programme in which the participant asks a question and answers it himself or herself. It is aimed at creating a new context of self-reflection and self-expression and facilitating a potential interaction between participants.

Abandoning the participant's individual traits, the 'SelfVoice' programme attempts to redefine the subtle and interesting relation-ship between participants and observers.

P200-P201
1. SelfVoice
© Xiao Wei
2. SelfVoice
© Xiao Wei
3. SelfVoice
© Xiao Wei

ZHANG Xiaotao:
Crawling through the Microscope

Zhang Xiaotao is an oddity among Chinese contemporary artists; many of his works are connected to the city and to the depths of his mind. His oddness is embodied in the uniqueness of his perspective. Few people can see and crawl through the world from the perspective of a tiny animal like he does; and the result is a series of microscopic images. He believes that his sensitivity has helped him to find a method and a means of expressing the macroscopic through the microscopic. For a long time he made works on canvas, occasionally putting out installations; but from 2007 his style underwent a massive change and, after about a year, he revealed the 32-minute animated film 'Mist' to the outside world.

This is a legend about animals building a huge steel factory along a river in a pastoral setting. It all sounds absurd, a scenario in which animals wage war against the backdrop of a steel mill. Following deaths, terror and struggles, during which the animals collectively descend into madness and collapse, the narrative becomes one of rebirth. On the ruins of the steel factory, the animals construct a 'Window of the World' theme park, eventually tearing it down to erect a Tower of Babel. In their process of demolition and reconstruction everything attains rebirth. Death and rebirth are connected. Zhang Xiaotao uses the fabled 'animal theatre' to present us with much of the fruitlessness, ignorance, arrogance and absurdity involved in the progress of materialism.

Ants are the stars of this animated film. Ants were the main motif in Zhang Xiaotao's earlier paintings and, when they appear in the film, they seem more magnificent. That is because the intelligence and power seen at work in their movements as a collective mass command respect. The ants link everything together, forming a grand narrative epic. As individuals, ants are insignificant, but as a group they can push mountains into the sea.

We see many shadows of the city in Zhang Xiaotao's work, but they are not the usual computer generated images of tiny tropical cities, nor are they the cities of the future posted at urban construction sites around China. They are a mix of the artist's growing experience and encounters in life, the anguish and dreams of China's era of drastic change.

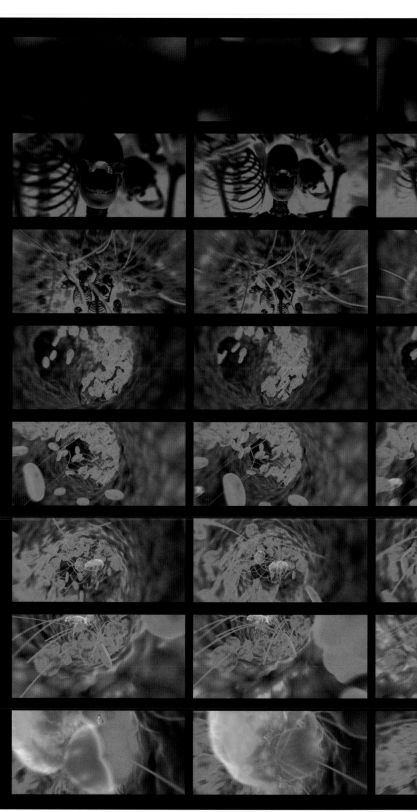

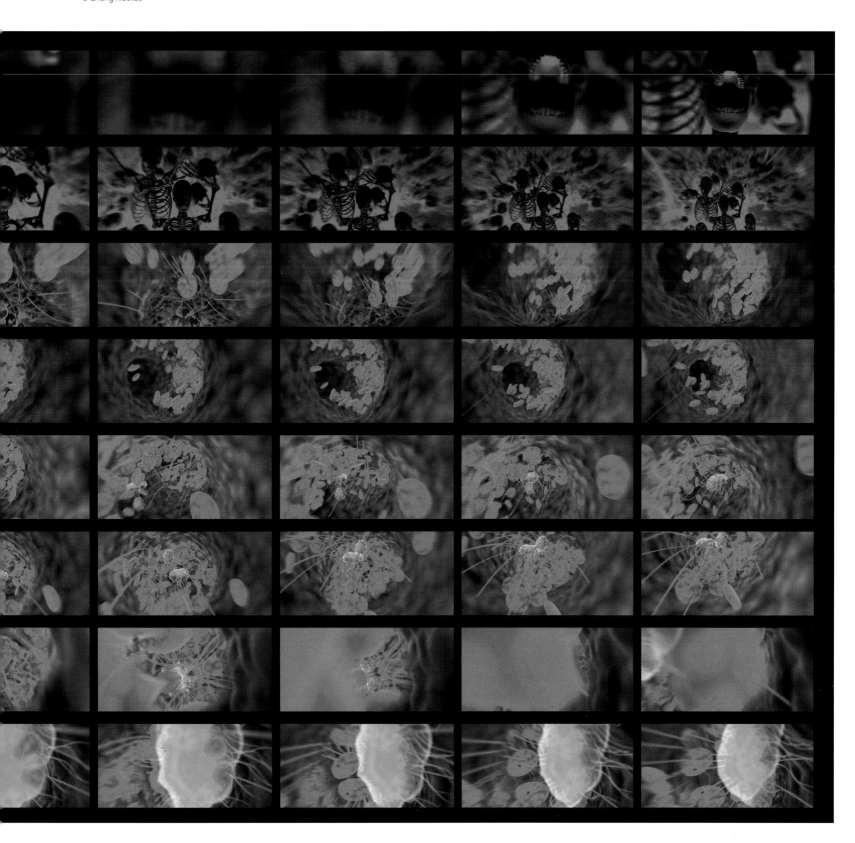

MIST

ARTIST: **Zhang Xiaotao**
PRODUCED: **2007–2008**
CATEGORY: **Animation**
LENGTH: **34'04"**
MATERIALS: **digital art**
Copyright © Zhang Xiaotao

DESCRIPTION I will use 'Mist' to construct a visualized logic of reflection, to once again decode or encode the process of spatiotemporal transition that we have gone through, spiritually and bodily, from hope to disillusionment to rebirth, from the modernization path of the Mao era to the contemporary scene, where the era of globalized liberal economics and post-socialist political society are intricately interwoven. I hope to use visualized language to probe the injuries and pains that afflict our bodies and souls, to probe the minuteness of the individual and the vastness of the times. We encounter these conundrums and pressures in every era, and it seems that in our historical experience, every time we encounter massive social change and destruction, Chinese culture comes out with a shocking ability to recover, so that our spiritual roots have never totally collapsed but continued on to this day through the impermanent cycles of the millennia. Rebirth and transmutation from destruction seems to be the religion that universally connects us as a people. There are always identical trends in history. Where are we in this fog-like labyrinth of the tangled mass of history and reality? Where is the world?

1

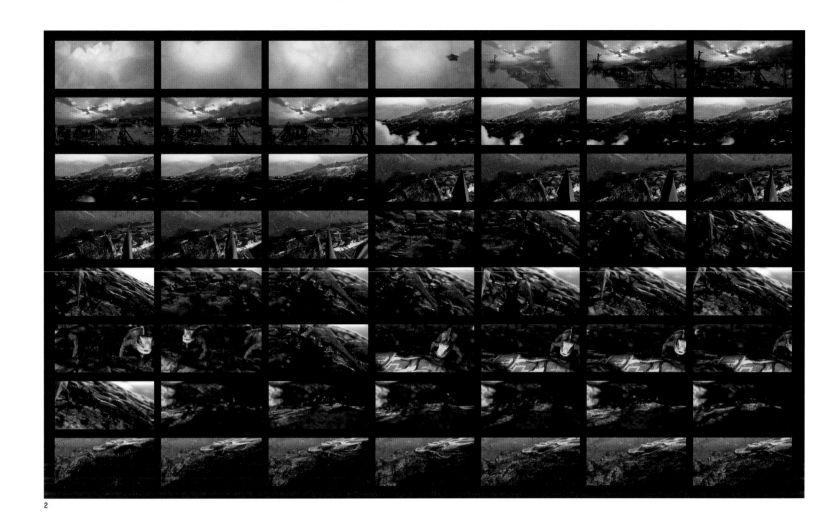

2

3

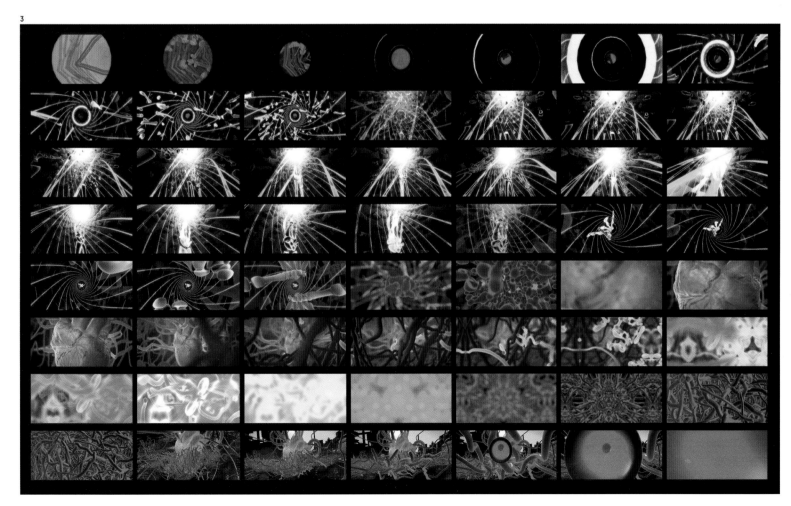

SOUND ART

YAN Jun

YAN Jun: 'Useful' and 'Useless' Fragments of Daily Life

Most people would acknowledge Yan Jun's great contribution when talking about sound art in China. He is a practising avant-garde musician, improviser and organizer of numerous art events. He is a practitioner of field recording and related sound artwork. He writes poetry, gives poetry readings, makes installations and runs an independent publishing company. Equipped with a portable recorder that he uses everyday, he has opened his mind to everything around him and has therefore accumulated a huge collection of 'useful' and 'useless' audio materials, which are in fact fragments of his daily life.

'Local Listening', created in 2009, is a sound installation containing forty field recordings. In fact many of Yan Jun's recent recordings, from 'Broken Loudhailer' to 'Silent Tribute for Earthquake', are from his everyday life experience. In 'Local Listening', forty headphones hang at different heights, mixing together a chaotic and subtle soundscape. Many movable blocks are put on the floor, which the audience must assemble and stand on, wearing the headphones to listen to individual sounds. In this game, the audience will put together their own new micro-geography and sound narrative.

According to Yan Jun, to choose is to engage in politics; and politics is poetry itself. The audience will create a microcosm out of their desire and their interactions.

LOCAL LISTENING

ARTIST: **Yan Jun**
PRODUCED: **2009**
MEDIA: **sound files, MP3 players, headphones, blocks**
Copyright © Yan Jun

P207
The tiny sounds collected from daily life, 2007–2008
© Yan Jun

P208-P209
1. The tiny sounds collected from daily life, 2007–2008
© Yan Jun
2. The tiny sounds collected from daily life, 2007–2008
© Yan Jun
3. Sound poetry performance, Peng Hao Theatre, Beijing, 2009
© Yan Jun

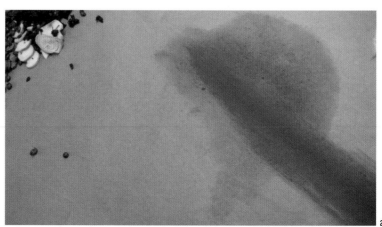

INDEX OF NAMES

Postface by FANG Zhenning

To begin this postface I would like to quote a recent article from my blog:

When I received the information about the Hu Huishan Memorial House from the architect Liu Jiakun, it was very close to the deadline for selecting exhibition works. But I wanted to include it, for it is a design that truly touches the hearts of visitors. This memorial may be the smallest in the world, for it was built to commemorate an ordinary child. It is located in a grove next to the 512 Exhibition Hall, part of the Jianchuan Museum Complex at Anren.

Fifteen-year-old Hu Huishan was a student at Juyuan Middle School, Dujiangyan. She died on 12 May 2008 in the Sichuan earthquake, one of thousands of child victims. How should we express our condolences? The architect Liu Jiakun found a way by designing a unique building just for her: the Hu Huishan Memorial House. He did what he could, while many other Chinese architects found their designs were unsuitable for reconstruction projects after the earthquake disaster. Although the work seems small, the designer's motivation is clear – his conscience – and it succeeds in stirring our souls more deeply than the announcements of death statistics.

A successful piece of architecture should be like a work of art. The difference between a good artwork and mediocre one is whether or not it touches the heart. I was so impressed when I first saw this house, that I had an impulse to plant a little pure-white flower in front of Hu Huishan Memorial. I feel that this memorial is not just for one young soul, but also for all the children who have died in disasters throughout the world. It respects and treasures ordinary lives. Jiakun's design will be the perfect way to end this catalogue, and it will give true meaning and a proper explanation of the theme of the exhibition – Heart-Made.

'Heart-Made' stands for work that is designed from the heart; ideal buildings and urban environments come from the heart. 'Heart-Made' implies that design should be driven by the heart, by the conscience. It reflects the moral principles of Chinese architects who are in the process of developing sustainable architectural design.

In July 2008, Fan Di'an, the Curator of the National Art Museum of China and the Chinese General Curator of this exhibition, called me and asked me to assist with this exhibition. His trust both pleased and surprised me. The exhibition would reveal the architectural design and construction achievements in China, which have already been in the spotlight of the world architectural industry, but it would also provide recognition for the Chinese architects' efforts. However, it is no easy task to single out a few works from so many achievements.

It would be impossible to expect one exhibition to reflect the whole panorama of Chinese architecture. Believing that the majority of audiences would be most interested in knowing more about the current state of Chinese architecture, I decided to limit the scope of the exhibition to works designed in the past decade. This also relates most closely to my own personal experience of recent developments and changes in Chinese cities and architecture, which are in a state of constant flux.

Ten years ago, having lived abroad for a long time, I decided to move back to Beijing for two reasons. Fourteen years ago I participated in the exhibition and seminar held by Rem Koolhaas in Tokyo, in which he spoke highly of contemporary China and predicted that Asia had a promising future. It was his forecast that broadened my horizons, although I still had no sense about the development of China. This alone, however, was not enough to encourage me to return. It was only in 2000, when I discovered that a private Chinese company, SOHO

China, had decided to build 'Commune by the foot of the Great Wall', and had proposed the concept of collecting architectural art, that I started to sense that an unprecedented era was approaching. As a Chinese architectural critic, unless I was based in China, I would surely be unqualified to comment on Chinese architecture. You can only witness history in the making when you are at the centre of things. The events of the past decade have confirmed that I made the right choice. Moreover, this exhibition and the catalogue constitute a summary of my observations about the recent changes in Chinese architecture and urbanism.

The rise of China is like a waking dragon, as is being demonstrated by the current and future development of China. This exhibition is only a sample from the vast amount of construction taking place in China. I adhered to a single principle when selecting works – the audience must sense and understand the immense enthusiasm and wisdom that lies behind the creativity of the new generation of Chinese architects.

Just as a building is the result of a successful cooperation, this exhibition and its catalogue are the products of many people's wisdom. I hereby thank all my partners for participating in this project. It could not have happened without the total confidence of the Chinese General Curator Fan Di'an. I have learned a great deal by taking up this opportunity. The Europalia 2009 committee exerted a positive influence on our team thanks to its exceptional organizational ability and professionalism. I would like to give special thanks to Christophe Pourtois and Marcelle Rabinowicz from CIVA, who cooperated with us not only by providing exhibition spaces, but also by their close involvement in the catalogue. They have demonstrated the importance that CIVA has attached to this event, by the great efforts that have been devoted to editing the catalogue and organizing the exhibition. Although I worked as an independent curator, for this project I was supervised by Chen Ping, who constantly reminded me of the exhibition's importance. He also helped me as far as possible with the difficulties inherent in curating an exhibition. Yan Dong, Wang Ying and Jiang He made all the arrangements for meetings between the Belgian and Chinese teams. Zheng Yan offered quiet and efficient support to the curators in charge of different aspects of the exhibition.

Another invisible team also contributed to this exhibition. Lin Fanyu, our initial exhibition assistant, worked actively and unselfishly, while Zhang Daping, who joined us in the later crucial stages, sacrificed almost all of her spare time for the exhibition. In the busiest period, we communicated with each other by MSN. Furthermore, there are others, such as translators, some of whom I have not even met, who have contributed to this project.

Finally, I would like to thank the architects and firms who accepted our invitation to take part in the exhibition, confirming the mutual trust and good relationships between architectural critics and architects. As far as possible, I have included the most up to date design projects in this exhibition and catalogue. For example, the cover image – 'Chongqing Urban Forest' – is the most ambitious and futuristic design yet produced by Ma Yansong and his MAD team. With a view of a cubic garden, this 380-metre-high skyscraper is regarded as the most pioneering creation yet made by any contemporary Chinese architect.

'Chongqing Urban Forest' is the first design by MAD that refers to the theory of 'high-density nature'. What does it mean? Perhaps it is the future of architecture? Be that as it may, it reminds me of the film *Why has Bodhi-Dharma Left for the East?* In fact, I am more than willing to regard it as the aura around a civilization in transition.

4 June 2009, Beijing

URBAN FOREST ARCHITECT: Ma Yansong / MAD

Published by Fonds Mercator, the CIVA and europalia.china in two thousand and nine.

Typeset in TSTAR by Dojo Design, Brussels
Book and cover designed by Dojo Design, Brussels

Printed on 170 g G-Print Grycksbo Paper and bound by Snel Grafics sa, Vottem